DIGITAL SCRAPBOOKING

JOHN SLATER

in
easy steps

BARNES & NOBLE BOOKS

NEW YORK

In easy steps is an imprint of Computer Step
Southfield Road · Southam
Warwickshire CV47 0FB · United Kingdom
www.ineasysteps.com

This edition published for Barnes & Noble Books, New York
FOR SALE IN THE USA ONLY
www.bn.com

Notice of Liability

Every effort has been made to ensure that this book contains accurate and
current information. However, Computer Step and the author shall not be
liable for any loss or damage suffered by readers as a result of any information
contained herein.

Acknowledgements and Trademarks
Cover image courtesy of Clara Wallace – MatterOfScrap.com (background),
John Slater(photo), Sean Gladwell (designer).

All trademarks are acknowledged as belonging to their respective companies.

Printed and bound in the United Kingdom

ISBN 0-7607-7860-4

Table of Contents

Images for the exercises

Regardless of the software you choose, the images shown on these pages are available for your use. They can be downloaded from the website www.ineasysteps.com. Save files in a specific location and consider making a folder especially for the exercises in this book. If you are using Photoshop Elements use the Organizer to store the downloads. You will need the files shown below if you want to follow the exercises exactly as described.

Alan	Auckland	Badge	Blueflowerspattern	Captain	Cardrona	Clara'spaper	clara-zebrastripes
Dad	Damaged	Diamondgrad	Faint	Faroes	Flag	Flower	Flowers
Foot	FourFairies	Frame	Greenwich	Gymnast	Hat	Hongi	IDCard
Jack	Kalahari	Kim1	Kim2	Kim3	Kim4	Lancaster	Logbook
Mac	Mates	Merrygoround	Navigate	Nik	Pattern	Postcard	Raffia
RedButton	Ruth&Garth	Soccer1	Soccer2	Streetwise	Stripey	Tag	Team
TeamSA	Teddy	ThreemoreFairies	Tiger	Tiles	TreeFairies	TwoFairies	Victoria

CREDITS

The author wishes to thank a long list of
people who have been kind enough to allow
use of personal photographs and have offered
help, advice and insight to the world of
scrapbooking.

Carolyn Lamb-Miller

Jackie Tyne

Debbie McRobie

Lisa Thornley

Janine Burgess

Sue Francis

Olivia Forbes

Vicki Turnbull

Paul Slater

Mark Gurnett

Patrick Lauson

Julie Dent

Malcolm Milburn

Rod Buick

A special thanks to Henry Francis and Clara Wallace who have made wonderful contributions
to the project sections at the end of the book. Lastly to Christine Hartley and Brenda
Christie, who have had the unenviable task of proof reading the manuscript, sincere thanks
and appreciation.

Introducing Digital Scrapbooking

Everyone has a story to tell. How will you tell yours? Digital scrapbooking takes traditional ideas and moves them into the 21st century. Scissors and glue are replaced by imaging software and the computer. The ideas are still the same; it's just the process that is different. From paint effects to photographic composition there are tips, exercises and projects here to develop your skills. This book will take you from being a novice digital scrapbooker to a good intermediate standard. It is hoped that this book will illuminate your ideas, eliminate some of the fear and frustration you may have with computers and, above all, introduce you to a fun and enjoyable pastime.

Covers

Chapter One

Jack.jpg

Getting Started

What do you need to get started with digital scrapbooking? As a bare minimum you need a computer and some imaging software. Just about any computer will do, PC or Macintosh. While this book concentrates on the PC, you can do all the projects on a suitably equipped Macintosh. Imaging software is the stuff that allows you to change or manipulate photos and make your own papers and embellishments. It also enables the creative use of text either as headlines or for journaling. For the more ambitious a scanner would be useful, and maybe a digital camera.

Much of the book is devoted to making "papers," "elements," "embellishments" or whatever word you use to describe the components of each page. At the initial stage it is appreciated that you may just want to add a few digital elements to a pre-existing base. If even this is too daunting, guidance is given on sourcing and using pre-made digital pages. Just add your photos and you are finished – nothing could be easier. Towards the end of the book, projects bring all these elements together to create finished layouts. Ultimately it is your ideas that matter and your ideas that determine what you need.

Basic Steps for any Digital Project

In reality the steps are little different from those of a traditional scrapbooking project. You are limited only by your own imagination.

1. Establish an idea and a basic layout. Some people find it an advantage to do this on paper

2. Translate the paper idea to the computer, decide what you can make yourself, and source ready-made elements

3. Collect your images, background papers and elements, and put them in a project folder

4. Scan additional images and elements

5. Crop, resize and correct all images

6. Assemble your layout, mats, borders, journaling etc

7. Reflect on the overall design and make any changes

8. Commit and know when to stop

Digital versus Traditional

If you surf scrapbooking websites or venture into scrapbooking retailers there appear to be two distinct camps – the traditional and the digital. There don't need to be, and this book makes no such distinction. Indeed, many of the ideas shown and described here owe their inspiration to scrapbookers who do not have any desire, now or in the future, to get in front of a computer screen.

Some people will find the computer an exciting place to be. Others may find it difficult. The best of both worlds can be had with just a little understanding and by combining both skills. Use the computer to enhance and develop traditional ideas, and with just a little know-how, you will be flying. This book aims to stimulate your imagination. Experimentation is the key to finding out what is possible. Do not be afraid to play – with digital you can always go backwards and undo!

Why go Digital? What are the Advantages?

It Can Be Cheaper   Initially digital scrapbooking will not save you money if you need to buy a computer and all the associated equipment. But if you already have a computer, all you need is the software and off you go. No need for boxes of bits and pieces all doing specific jobs: the software has flexible alternatives already built in. Importantly, making mistakes does not affect your wallet – just undo and try again. Photos do not have to be cut up or extra copies made.

You'll Save on Paper   Traditional scrapbooking paper has a one-time use. Digital files can be used over and over again. You can buy inexpensive pre-made digital paper or create your own from scratch – essentially this is free. With digital there are no wastage and storage problems. It is, perhaps, too easy to go into a shop and buy a bundle of exciting-looking but expensive papers and either never use them or get them damaged with spilled tea. It must happen all the time. Own up! Don't forget that you can create and print unique pages for your traditional album from your computer.

No Need for Glues and Adhesives   Not only can these be messy, they are not necessary. Digital files can be assembled or disassembled with ease. Traditional album pages have to be ripped apart to recover or change any of the images.

Save on Storage   Store designs on the computer and get rid of those cupboards full of junk. And what about those boxes under the bed?

Pens, Cutters and Stencils are Unnecessary   There is no need to buy any of these gadgets – similar tools already exist in the software. Customize these tools to create a huge variety of pens, brushes, shape cutters or stencils. Sophistication is easy. Traditional scrappers could utilize this amazing ability to make unusual shapes or fantastic textures and incorporate these into their own traditional designs. The rewards are both creative and financial.

You Can Still Make Albums   It may be argued that there is no need for albums as layouts can be viewed on screen or via the internet. The opinion expressed in this book is that the printed page is still needed and encouraged. Scrappers still want to hold the image but prints have the advantage of not being "lumpy bumpy" – there is no relief, no thick embellishments, that can damage other pages.

No Mess or Wastage   Digital allows you to re-use your materials time and time again. This doesn't mean all your layouts will look the same, as all elements can be changed very easily. It takes just a few seconds to change a gingham paper from blue to red. It is hard to damage a digital file. Gone are the frustrations of creases, torn edges or papers covered with breakfast, all of which waste money.

Sharing and Transportability   Replicate your pages for friends all over the world and share them using the power of the internet. Going digital means that you can share designs easily with your friends, but please never claim fame for the elements if they came from elsewhere. Give credit where it is due and be aware of copyright issues.

Practicality   You can do things that would be impossible by traditional methods. Blending images is so creative. Vignettes are perfect for heritage layouts – impossible in a traditional album. Match and change colors with simplicity. Resize and reshape your pictures easily. Use scanned sections of diaries, journals and logbooks, and keep the valuable originals safe and in pristine condition – you couldn't put these in the album anyway!

Imaging Software

Importantly, imaging software offers lots of new creative possibilities that are impossible to achieve using traditional methods. All scrapbooking enthusiasts can benefit from an understanding of digital techniques. If you are a traditional scrapbooker you will be amazed by the new opportunities presented by the digital format and you can incorporate many ideas into your traditional layouts. You will experience not only how to make albums on the computer but how to change and create individual components.

Just about any imaging software will be able to cope with digital scrapbooking. Of course some will do the job better than others and only the top software will be able to offer the most advanced effects. Still, it is surprising what you can do with very basic programs and, more and more, these are becoming dedicated or have dedicated sections for the digital scrapbooker. This book concentrates on Photoshop Elements and Photoshop. Other versions of these programs work in a very similar way. You should, however, be able to follow and complete most of the exercises and projects in this book regardless of the software you use.

Photoshop Elements

Adobe Photoshop Elements is the world's best selling image editing program. Although designed for the home user the software has many powerful features. This program provides the basis for much of this book so a brief introduction is in order. When you start Elements you have to choose what you want to do. Essentially there are four starting points. Choose as follows:

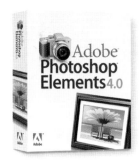

If you are a Mac user iPhoto does virtually the same job as the Organizer. For additional help and lots of inspiration you should explore the Getting Started file on the CD and regularly look at the Help files. Not only will they solve many problems, they will also provide many interesting ideas.

1. The Organizer to manage and sort your images, and importantly help you find them. You should use the Organizer to store the images available for the exercises included in this book.

2. A powerful image editing program that has many of the sophisticated tools found in Photoshop. Elements uses the same tools but with a simple straightforward interface. You will use the Editor to enhance your photos and repair old damaged ones before putting them into your scrapbook pages. Image editing techniques are illustrated in Chapter 8.

3. A Creations wizard that guides you through the steps needed to make albums, slide shows, collages, calendars, cards, online galleries and CDs. You will be guided through the process in Chapter 9.

4. Start from scratch. Virtually all of the exercises and projects will start from a blank page.

Photoshop

Photoshop is the premier professional image editing program from Adobe and can rightly claim to be the world standard. Everything you can do with Photoshop Elements you can do with Photoshop – but more so. Photoshop really is the big brother of Photoshop Elements. Essentially the instructions you see in this book will be very similar for all versions of Photoshop going back to version 5. Rarely are there any significant differences in process – but when these do occur you will be made aware of them. Sometimes it is assumed that you are clever enough to appreciate that Window > Color Swatches in Photoshop Elements is the same as Window > Swatches in Photoshop. There are quite a few of these palette and name differences, but rest assured the commands are the same.

Paint Shop Pro

Paint Shop Pro is a fully featured program that many consider to be the rival of Photoshop but at a fraction of the price. Of particular interest to digital scrapbookers are the Xtras available specifically for digital scrapbooking. These pre-made digital elements are extensive in range. Many can be utilized by other programs and are worth considering if you want someone else to do all the designing while you stick with creating layouts. The "Sampler Series" is a worthy starting point. This collection of heritage, fun, shabby and elegant themes provides you with templates, backgrounds and embellishments, and gives you the opportunity to sample the themes featured throughout the series.

Scrapbook Factory

Scrapbook Factory is probably the best dedicated scrapbook software currently available. This software will be well suited to users who prefer to assemble pages using pre-designed layouts. Scrapbook Factory Deluxe offers an extensive collection of 5,000+ exclusive templates to create scrapbooks and other keepsake projects as well as a digital photo editor to ensure  that your photos look their absolute best. The software also offers sophisticated drawing tools along with thousands of graphics and photorealistic elements designed to enhance virtually any layout.

Hewlett-Packard Creative Scrapbook Assistant

At the opposite end of the scale is Creative Scrapbook Assistant. This is not quite as dedicated to scrapbooking as the name suggests and can only be recommended for users who only wish to dabble. Serious users can spend just a little more money and get a much more sophisticated program.

Other Software and Free Trials

Other software that will work well is Corel Photo Paint, ULead Photo Impact and Microsoft's Digital Image Suite. Many companies offer 30-day free trials of their software so you can try before you buy:

www.adobe.com (Photoshop and Photoshop Elements)

www.corel.com (Corel Draw suite, Corel Painter, Paint Shop Pro)

www.ulead.com (PhotoImpact)

www.novadevelopment.com (clip art)

Understand your Workspace

Photoshop Elements and Windows

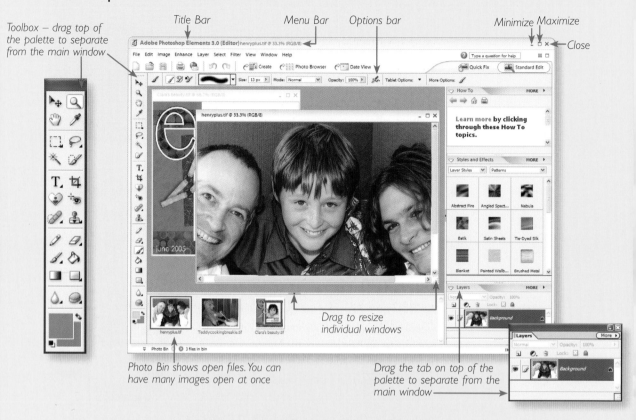

Title Bar

Menu Bar

Options bar

Minimize Maximize

Close

Toolbox – drag top of the palette to separate from the main window

Drag to resize individual windows

Photo Bin shows open files. You can have many images open at once

Drag the tab on top of the palette to separate from the main window

Understand your Keyboard

Many of Photoshop's commands require you to press certain keys or combinations of keys. Some like Alt/Option are keys you may never have used before. Check that you know where to find these.

Backspace/Delete

Delete

Esc

Caps lock

Shift

Control Command

Alt/Option

Enter/Return

Arrow/Nudge keys

Why use Layers?

One of the principal building blocks of imaging software is the use of layers. You will need both an appreciation and an understanding of layers to be at your most creative.

To understand layers better take a look at a traditional scrapbook and compare it with a computer layout of the same page. There really is not that much difference. Assembling a traditional page is the same as building elements using individual layers on the computer. Virtually all the projects and exercises in this book will use layers.

Traditional Scrapbook Layout

In a traditional album you start a new project by turning to a blank page. On this page you put decorated paper or several papers torn into shapes or strips. This is the base of your creation and it covers the white background. On top of this you would add a picture or two, maybe a mat for journaling, a couple of embellishments and maybe some title text. Each of these objects is moved around until the whole "collage" looks good. Only then do you glue or stick down the individual objects.

Digital Layouts are Little Different

In a digital layout you start with a blank file, which the software calls Background. You add several objects onto this page, stacked on top of one another, just as you would in a traditional scrapbook. If you use layers, each object can be moved and re-arranged, as in a traditional album, but additionally images and elements can be resized, blended and manipulated in situ. When you are satisfied with your layout you can merge layers or "flatten" the layers, just like gluing down in an album.

In fact if you think like a traditional scrapbooker then digital is entirely logical. The steps are the same – only digital offers more scope. Layers offer flexibility. Working without layers is like trying to walk with your feet tied together. Understand layers and you have a cupboard full of creative possibilities that are the envy of the traditionalists. Layers can make the impossible idea possible.

Layers – Make them your Friend

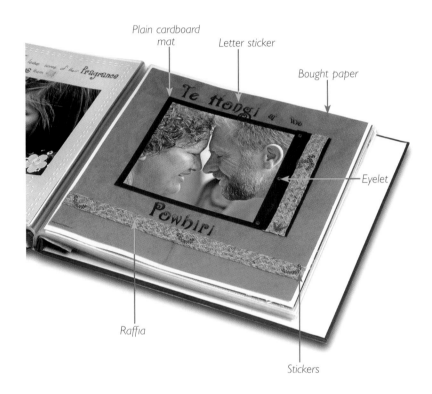

Plain cardboard mat

Letter sticker

Bought paper

Eyelet

Raffia

Stickers

Traditional Scrapbook Album

(Courtesy Carolyn Lamb-Miller)

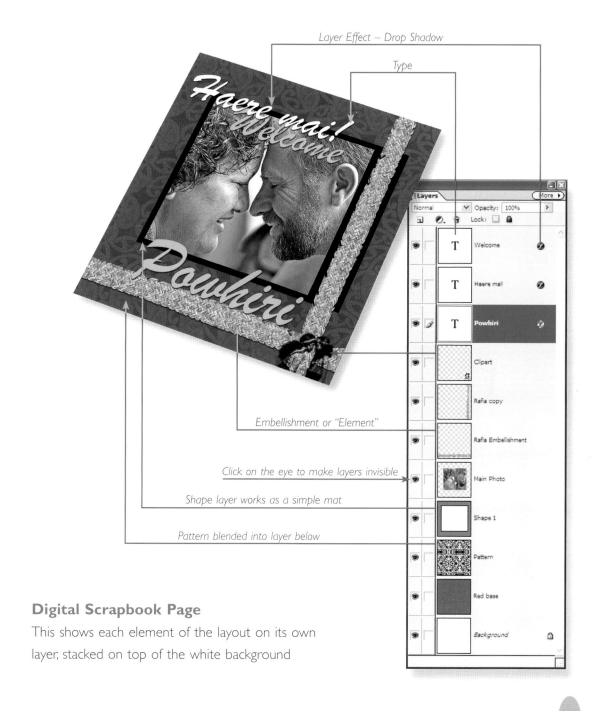

Layer Effect – Drop Shadow

Type

Embellishment or "Element"

Click on the eye to make layers invisible

Shape layer works as a simple mat

Pattern blended into layer below

Digital Scrapbook Page

This shows each element of the layout on its own
layer, stacked on top of the white background

Undo History

Jack.jpg©Rod Buick

We all make mistakes. Have you ever made a traditional album and stuck something down only to regret it five minutes later? With digital this is unlikely to be a problem. All designs should be fluid, so don't be afraid of experimenting; you can't hurt yourself, and you can't hurt the computer. Encourage yourself to play. All can be undone! Most computer programs offer Edit > Undo to get yourself out of trouble. Better are programs like Photoshop Elements and Photoshop that allow multiple undos to step back three, four or even twenty steps, as you will soon see. This short exercise shows how you can experiment without "causing the world to end".

Make Friends with the Undo History Palette

Images can be downloaded from www.ineasysteps. com, but this exercise can be done with any image.

1 Start Photoshop Elements and open the file Jack.jpg (File > Open) and the Undo History palette (Window > Undo History)

2 From the menu choose Image > Rotate > 90° Right. The image rotates and an entry appears in the Undo History palette. Repeat the process. The image is now upside down

In Photoshop the palette is simply called History. In both cases the default number of states shown in the palette is 20. This is quickly used up as an entry appears each time you press OK or Enter, or click with the mouse. The recommendation is to change this to at least 50 using Preferences: Edit > Preferences > General.

3 From the menu choose Image > Rotate > Flip Vertical, and then Flip Horizontal. The image returns to its original position

4 From the menu choose Enhance > Auto Smart Fix. The dark shadows lighten slightly, and another entry appears

5 Choose Enhance > Adjust Color > Remove Color. The image changes to grayscale. Assume you've made a mistake. Choose Edit > Undo Remove Color. The palette automatically steps back to the previous entry. For multiple undos just click on the relevant entry in the palette. Click on the Open entry to return to the start image

The keyboard shortcut for undo is Ctrl + Z.

6 From the menu choose Filter > Stylize > Solarize. All entries are removed except the new one. Save the file if you wish, and close it

All entries in the Undo History palette are lost when the file is closed.

If any palette is too small it can be extended by dragging downwards from the bottom right corner.

When you step back with the Undo History, later actions are grayed out. If you make another change these entries are eliminated – this cannot be undone. Some programs like Photoshop offer more sophisticated undo controls and you can even save your actions to a text file for later reference.

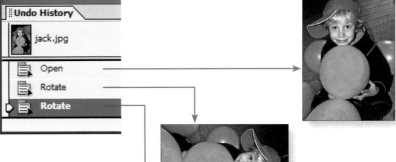

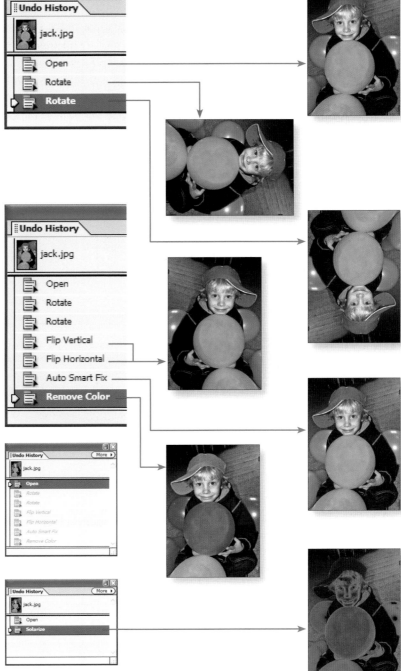

Understand Color

This book makes no pretence of turning you into a designer, but a few tips about color will help you put together more cohesive-looking layouts. Once you have decided upon an idea you will already have a feeling for the colors you will use. In some of the exercises you will pick specific colors that work well together – but how do you pick those colors? Guesswork? Trial and error? Neither! Science comes to your aid in the form of the Color Wheel. Certain color combinations always work well. Appreciate that primary colors of red, blue and yellow are full of energy and are frequently used for children's pages or sport. Secondary colors of violet, green and orange are just a little less intense and these find favor for special events such as parties. Perhaps easier to grasp is the use of warm or cold colors. It seems obvious to use cool blues for a skiing holiday while a trip to the Grand Canyon is more likely to convey the right message by being based around warm reds and yellows.

Color Wheel

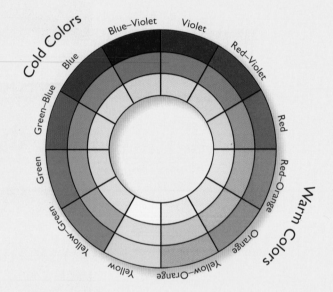

Monochromatic color is simple and classical. Tints of the same color work well to create a harmonious layout

Analogous color uses three colors next to each other, and again creates harmony and definite mood

Complementary color uses opposites on the wheel to add vibrancy. One color is dominant while the other adds contrast. Use for strong and exciting layouts

The Triad or three-color scheme uses colors at 120° apart on the wheel. This is the most daring scheme to adopt, so use it with care

Make & Change Simple Backgrounds

This is where you start to learn the basic techniques for digital scrapbooking. These are the same techniques that you use to correct or enhance your photos, make greetings cards and create calendars. It's only the end result that is different.

Initially you will discover how to make a new page and add basic color, basic texture and simple gradients. Importantly, bear in mind how you are going to present your pages – will you put them in traditional albums or are you limited to a size that the printer can print?

Covers

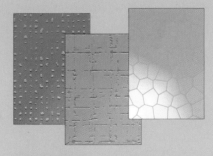

Diamondgrad.jpg   Stripey.jpg

Foot.jpg

Make a New Page

Digital scrapbooking is much easier to understand if you relate the computer processes directly to traditional techniques. When you start a new project in a traditional album you turn to a blank page. On the computer you simply create a blank page. All the exercises and projects in this book will start this way and it is strongly recommended that you adopt this approach with your own work. It is a big mistake to spend lots of time on an image and then try to make it fit the paper. Start with a blank piece of paper the size of your final print. Ask yourself "what is the maximum size of paper my printer can use?". This done, you will then discover how to add basic colors and textures to this page. Enjoy and have fun!

Set the Resolution to 300 pixels per inch for prints and 72 pixels per inch if you are going to make web pages.

File > New > Blank File

You have to start sometime! All programs will be similar. Normally you will see File > New and you will get a choice of preset blank file sizes. If the size you want does not exist you will have to enter the dimensions yourself. This will be the case if you want to make your pages the traditional 12 inch square size. Sometimes you will get a startup screen with several choices. Below is the startup screen for Photoshop Elements. Simply choose the Start From Scratch option to get the file size list. Try this out.

In this book Resolution will always be in pixels/inch not pixels/cm. If you make a mistake in this, the easiest solution is to close the file you are working on and start again.

Choose Letter or A4 size. This will give you a blank page in Portrait Mode. Make a mental note of the size of the paper. Knowing how big your page is will help avoid unexpected problems when you scan or bring in your digital photos

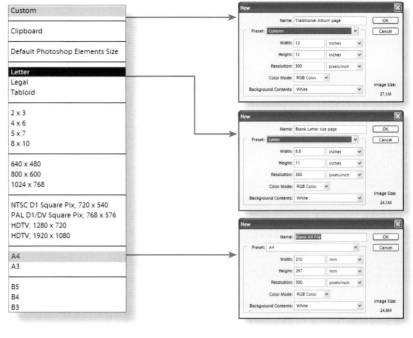

The projects at the end of this book are based around the traditional 12 inch square page. The exercises and mini projects in the rest of the book use a variety of the available preset pages. Letter size paper is common in the USA and A4 is widely used throughout the rest of the world.

Some programs allow you to save a custom size. The one shown left is from Photoshop. When you view the drop-down list the new size appears near the top of the list

2 If you want a Landscape shaped page you need to turn your page (often referred to as the Canvas) using Image > Rotate > 90° Left

3 If you make a traditional or mini album the new page will be a twelve-inch or six-inch square. Close the file: File > Close

Portrait Page

Landscape Page

Square Page

Add & Change Page Colors

Here you will make very simple backgrounds. In later chapters you will have the opportunity to create more complex backgrounds. There are many ways to choose your paint colors.

Color Swatches

1 Make a new file with the dimensions shown below

You can use any size file you like for these exercises. Avoid excessively large files as this will slow down your computer.

2 To color this page with plain color is very simple. First choose the color. In the menu choose Window > Color Swatches

In Photoshop the menu command is simply Window > Swatches.

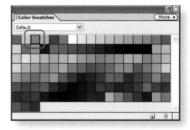

3 Click on the third square along and notice that the foreground color square in the Toolbox changes to this green color

4 Pick the Paintbucket in the Toolbox. Put the mouse in the empty page and click. Your page will be filled with the green color

The Paintbucket always uses the foreground color.

5 Click on the Switch Colors arrow (see top of next page). The green becomes the background color

6 Click on the second square along to make the foreground color yellow

7 Click in the page again to change the color to yellow

8 The Toolbox colors should now look like this:

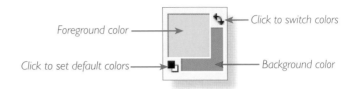

Foreground color ⟶

Click to switch colors

Click to set default colors ⟶

Background color

Color Picker

Some programs like Photoshop have a specific Color palette for the visual mixing of colors. Less advanced programs have more limited options but this is still more than adequate for most scrapbookers.

The Swatches palette may not include the exact colors you want for your album page. Specific colors can easily be chosen with the Color Picker.

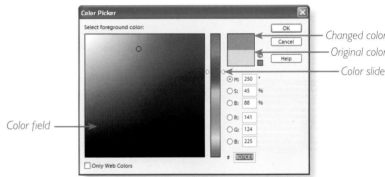
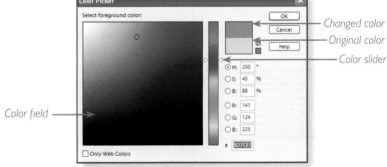

Changed color

Original color

Color slider

Color field ⟶

While you are likely to set colors visually, be aware that colors can be specified numerically as shown in the right side of the Color Picker.

1 To show the Color Picker and change the foreground color just click in the foreground color square in the Toolbox

2 Move the white triangle sliders and/or click inside the color slider box to get approximately the color you want

3 Move your mouse inside the Color field and click to get a specific color. The new and original colors are compared in the top right corner of the Picker

4 Choose a blue color and fill your page

Add Colors to the Swatches Palette

When you are working on a project you may find it easier to store your own individual colors in the Color Swatches palette rather than create the color each time you want to use it.

1 Make sure you can see the Swatches palette and that the foreground color is similar to the blue shown previously

In addition to the techniques described, exact colors can be picked from photos using the Eyedropper Tool. You will see how this works in Chapter 4.

2 Move your mouse to the empty space at the bottom of the palette and the Paintbucket icon appears. Just click to add the new color to the palette

3 Give the new color a name as shown below

All the colors in the Swatches palette have names. Keep the mouse stationary over any swatch for a couple of seconds to reveal its name.

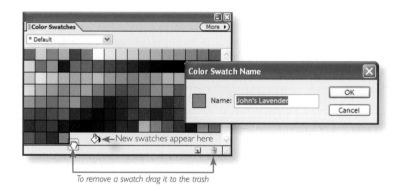

To remove a swatch drag it to the trash

Reset Colors

The default colors for the background and foreground squares are black and white. The easiest way to reset to black and white is to click on the small default color boxes to the left of the background color square

Default foreground color ——

Click to set default colors ——→

←—— Default background color

Gradient Tool

Gradient Tool Option Bar

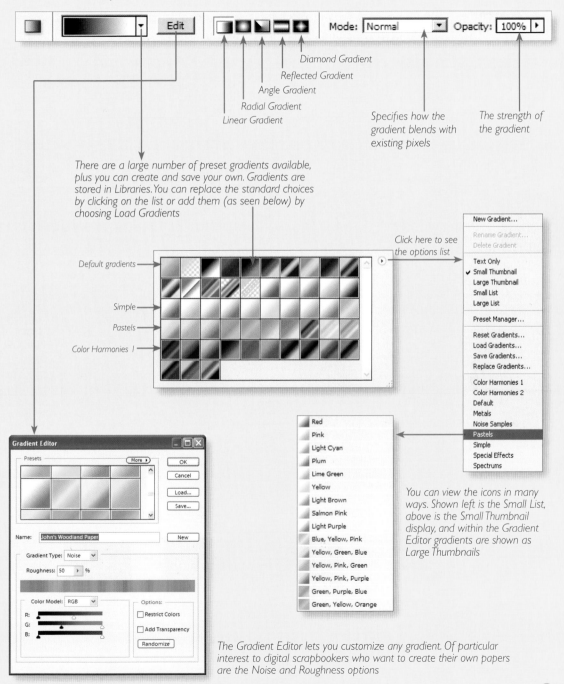

Diamond Gradient

Reflected Gradient

Angle Gradient

Radial Gradient

Linear Gradient

Specifies how the gradient blends with existing pixels

The strength of the gradient

There are a large number of preset gradients available, plus you can create and save your own. Gradients are stored in Libraries. You can replace the standard choices by clicking on the list or add them (as seen below) by choosing Load Gradients

Click here to see the options list

Default gradients

Simple

Pastels

Color Harmonies 1

New Gradient...

Rename Gradient...
Delete Gradient

Text Only
✓ Small Thumbnail
Large Thumbnail
Small List
Large List

Preset Manager...

Reset Gradients...
Load Gradients...
Save Gradients...
Replace Gradients...

Color Harmonies 1
Color Harmonies 2
Default
Metals
Noise Samples
Pastels
Simple
Special Effects
Spectrums

Red
Pink
Light Cyan
Plum
Lime Green
Yellow
Light Brown
Salmon Pink
Light Purple
Blue, Yellow, Pink
Yellow, Green, Blue
Yellow, Pink, Green
Yellow, Pink, Purple
Green, Purple, Blue
Green, Yellow, Orange

You can view the icons in many ways. Shown left is the Small List, above is the Small Thumbnail display, and within the Gradient Editor gradients are shown as Large Thumbnails

Gradient Editor

Presets   More ▶

OK
Cancel
Load...
Save...

Name: John's Woodland Paper   New

Gradient Type: Noise ▾

Roughness: 50 ▶ %

Color Model: RGB ▾

R:
G:
B:

Options:
☐ Restrict Colors
☐ Add Transparency
Randomize

The Gradient Editor lets you customize any gradient. Of particular interest to digital scrapbookers who want to create their own papers are the Noise and Roughness options

Adding Gradients to the Page

The Gradient Tool offers amazing possibilities for your backgrounds. Initially you apply a simple graded color to the page but this process evolves effortlessly into a sophisticated background worthy of gracing any album. This exercise will concentrate on the Linear Gradient. The Gradient Tool comes in five flavors. Experiment with each to discover the impact they can have on your album pages. Specialized gradients are explained in more detail when you make your own papers in Chapter 5.

Make the Grade

By default the gradient blends from the foreground color to the background color, but many other options are available. If you are working methodically through this exercise the gradient should now be black to white.

1 You may still have a page open.

If not, make one with the dimensions shown on page 26

2 Pick the Gradient Tool. In the Options bar you will see a preview of the present gradient. If you are following the exercise this will be black to white. Next to this preview are five buttons for the different gradient tools. From left to right these are:

>Linear
>Radial
>Angle
>Reflected
>Diamond

In Photoshop the Gradient Tool "lives" in the same space as the Paintbucket.

3 Pick the Linear Gradient. This creates a straightforward grade between two points. The points are decided by you. In this case click on the top of your page, hold down the mouse and drag to the bottom of the page. A line appears as you drag and the complete page is covered with a gradual black to white gradient

The gradient blend is controlled by the length of the line you drag, where the line starts and where the line ends. Longer lines give gentler gradients

...cont'd

Note that the Options bar changes as different tools are chosen. The Gradient Tool has a preview of the gradient that will be applied.

4 Select Edit > Undo to remove the gradient

5 Repeat the process several times, adjusting your start position and the length of the line. Notice how you can control the sharpness of the blend between the two colors

6 Change the colors to your own preference and draw the lines again, but this time try drawing in a horizontal direction or diagonally. Experiment with the other gradients. The examples shown below were made with the Radial gradient

7 Now find out what gradients are available in the different Libraries. Click on the small down arrow ▼ in the Options bar and then the right-pointing arrow in the top right corner of the next palette ⊙. A list of options and Libraries is revealed as shown on page 29

8 Experiment with the choices available and then close the file

In this exercise gradients are applied to the whole page. Selections (see next page) allow you to control the areas to be changed.

Green, Purple, Blue Pastel   *Russell's Rainbow from Special Effects*

The Magic Wand

As your skills develop you will find that there is a need to change part of an image and not the whole. You will need to learn how to make "selections". Once made, a selection restricts any changes you make to that area. Importantly, parts of the image not selected will remain unaltered. The selection tools are the Marquees, Lassos and the Magic Wand.

Although a favorite of many beginners, the Magic Wand tool should only be considered as a basic selection tool. The "magic" is particularly potent with images that have flat or gently graded colors or tones. Line drawings are an obvious example – being essentially black or white. Click on any white pixel and all other white pixels will be selected until a barrier is reached – the black lines act as a barrier. See this happen when working through the next exercise.

Magic Wand Options bar

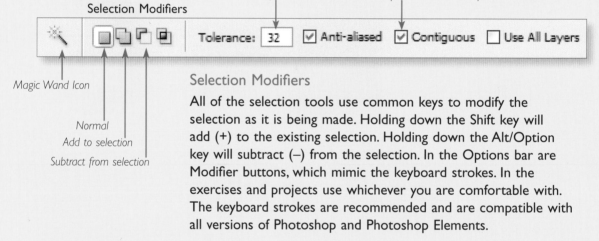

Selection Modifiers

All of the selection tools use common keys to modify the selection as it is being made. Holding down the Shift key will add (+) to the existing selection. Holding down the Alt/Option key will subtract (−) from the selection. In the Options bar are Modifier buttons, which mimic the keyboard strokes. In the exercises and projects use whichever you are comfortable with. The keyboard strokes are recommended and are compatible with all versions of Photoshop and Photoshop Elements.

The wand selects similar colors or tones according to the tolerance set in the Options bar. In effect, you can fine tune how the tool works. The choice is between 0 and 255. At the low values, say 10, the wand is very sensitive and will only select very similar colors or tones. At high values (over 100) a much broader range of colors and tones, perhaps too many, will be selected. Large settings are not recommended. The normal or default setting is 32.

To change the tolerance value click on the Magic Wand in the Toolbox. The Options bar for this tool will appear. Set the value – use the lowest value possible as this will give more precise selections. With high settings some unwanted parts of the image may be selected, but at normal view you may not see this happen.

Poor or sloppy selections will cause your image to deteriorate – so take a little time and care. As you work through this book you will find that selections become more and more difficult to make if you only use the Magic Wand. Other methods are waiting to be discovered.

Test your Gradient Skills

Foot.jpg

In this short exercise you will test your skills with the Gradient tools and start to make a drawing of a paper pattern look somewhat more realistic. This will prepare you for making more complex backgrounds later in the chapter. You will also develop your understanding of basic selections. Selection tools allow you to choose which area of an image receives the effect you want – you don't always want an effect everywhere on your album page. This paper pattern was bought in north-western China from the Tu people. They are famous for their embroidery – even on the soles of their shoes!

1   Open the image Foot.jpg. This has been scanned and corrected for you. In later chapters you will discover how to do this yourself

2   Take a close look at the image. It essentially consists of two flowers, several bits of foliage and a background. Initially you will select the background area and fill with a solid color

You are trying to color individual items so remember to select them first. If you don't, the whole of your image may be affected. If this happens don't panic, just use Edit > Undo.

3   Pick the Magic Wand tool. This is a great tool for simple images. It allows you to tell the computer which areas to change. Click in the space outside the foot shape. You will see two sets of moving dotted lines or "marching ants". These indicate the area selected – parts of the image that you can change. Areas not selected will NOT be changed by your next action

4   Pick a pale yellow color from the Swatches palette; shown here is Pastel Yellow which is the third yellow in the palette

The Magic Wand is a very simple tool. It works at its best with images that consist of simple colors – it will not work very efficiently with photographs.

All commands have keyboard shortcuts. To fill the area with color without clicking on the Paintbucket, use the Alt/Option + Backspace keys.

5 Pick the Paintbucket and click inside the selection. The area will change to the chosen yellow color

6 Now for something a little more creative. Make sure that your foreground and background colors are yellow and white. Zoom into the bigger of the two flowers on the drawing and with the Magic Wand click inside one of the petals. Only part of the flower is selected

7 Add to the selection using the selection modifier techniques shown on page 32

The Paintbucket has a built-in "magic wand" and will automatically fill in areas without the need for a selection. It is, however, recommended that you make a selection first: then you know which areas are going to be changed before you change them.

8 Pick the Radial Gradient and drag a line to apply the gradient. The length of the line and order of the colors will affect your result as shown below

Original

Gradient dragged within the selection

Gradient dragged outside the selection for softer results

Colors reversed and gradient dragged outside the selection.

The Zoom Tool

Zoom Tool Options bar

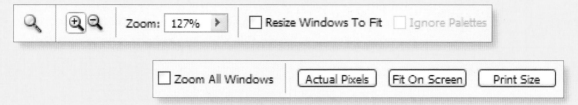

The Zoom Tool allows you to get close to your image and see exactly what it is made of. Magnify all images, especially when you are retouching, painting or trying to arrange a layout accurately.

To get a basic understanding, pick the Zoom Tool in the Toolbox. Move the mouse over any image and see the cursor change to a plus sign (+). Click on the center of the image and the magnification will increase or, in other words, you zoom in. Click again and again until the (+) sign in the cursor disappears. You are now at maximum magnification. Look in the Title Bar at the top of the screen and you will see that the magnification is 1600%.

At this point you will see that the image is made up of little squares. These are picture elements or PIXELS – each one a specific color. All digital images are made of these pixels. Whenever you change anything in a Photoshop image all you are really doing is changing the color of these pixels. It's a bit like "Painting by Numbers" but on a grand scale. Double-click on the Hand tool and the image reverts back to its original size.

The Navigator

(Window > Navigator)

An alternative to the Zoom is the Navigator. This lets you adjust the image's magnification and area of view. Change the magnification of your image by dragging the zoom slider, clicking the Zoom Out or Zoom In buttons, or typing a value in the text box. Drag the red view box in the thumbnail to move around your image.

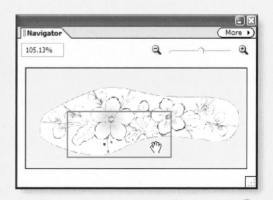

Hue/Saturation Command

Stripey.jpg

As a traditional scrapbooker you may have found the perfect paper from one of the many suppliers. If you want to use this in your own digital layouts it is a simple matter to scan the paper and create a digital file. Better still, you can alter the color subtly to match your existing content, or make dramatic changes. You can even create your own collection by making one design and changing the colors – which is what you will do here. The sample has already been made. It is probably a little too saturated for most people's taste but will allow a very clear demonstration of the possibilities. In Chapter 5 you will make more subtle papers from scratch.

Images from this book are available for you to download (see page 185) from www.ineasysteps.com.

Change existing backgrounds

1 Open the file Stripey.jpg. This sample has been made entirely within Photoshop Elements

If you change any commercially available paper just remember that this is for your own use only. Any other use may infringe Copyright laws.

2 From the menu choose Enhance > Adjust Color > Adjust Hue/Saturation. The Hue/Saturation dialog box appears

Hue/Saturation adjusts the hue (color), saturation (purity), and lightness of an image. Use the Saturation slider to make colors more vivid or more muted. Take care with the Lightness control as this can make images look very flat or "washed-out"

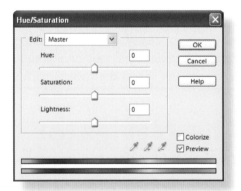

3 Experiment by moving the three sliders, saving any files you find interesting. For more control click on the Edit box and discover that you can limit your changes to just a part of the color spectrum. Examples are shown on the next page

Sometimes colors are not quite what they seem. Greens in particular may respond better to changes using Yellows in the Edit box.

Edit set to Master. Only the Lightness value is increased

Edit set to Master. The Hue value is moved to the left

Edit set to Master. The Hue value is moved to the right

Master	Ctrl+~
Reds	Ctrl+1
Yellows	Ctrl+2
Greens	Ctrl+3
Cyans	Ctrl+4
Blues	Ctrl+5
Magentas	Ctrl+6

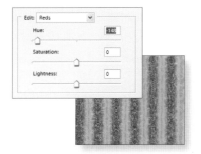

Edit set to Reds. Only the Red hues are changed

Edit set to Reds. The Hue value is moved to the right and Lightness increased

Master	Ctrl+~
Reds	Ctrl+1
Yellows	Ctrl+2
Greens	Ctrl+3
Cyans	Ctrl+4
Blues	Ctrl+5
Magentas	Ctrl+6

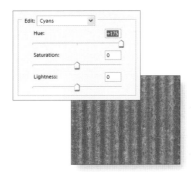

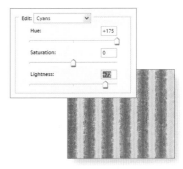

Edit set to Cyans. Only the Cyan hues are changed

Edit set to Cyans. The Hue value is moved to the right and Lightness increased

Easy Textured Backgrounds

Diamondgrad.jpg

Filters make adding textures to pages very easy. In fact the possibilities are endless and you may well find yourself having hours of fun just making backgrounds using all the amazing filters on offer.

Here you see a selection of ten backgrounds all originating from the same simple file and all taking just a couple of minutes to create. The power of digital scrapbooking is shown at its best! You will be walked through the easy-peazy process on page 40. For now just have fun looking at the images.

The original file is nothing more than a simple gradient. Full images are shown in the sidebar with enlarged sections below. The captions show which filters were used and the chosen settings.

The power of Filters

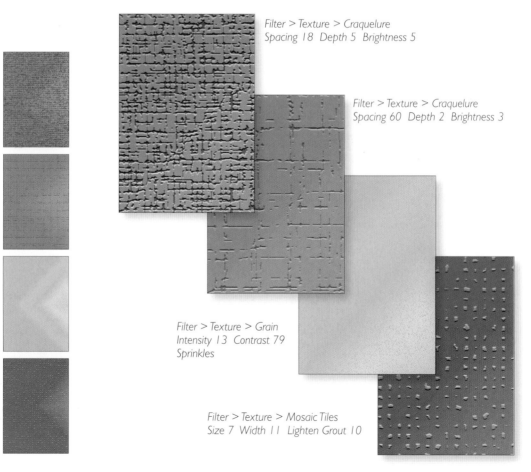

Filter > Texture > Craquelure
Spacing 18 Depth 5 Brightness 5

Filter > Texture > Craquelure
Spacing 60 Depth 2 Brightness 3

Filter > Texture > Grain
Intensity 13 Contrast 79
Sprinkles

Filter > Texture > Mosaic Tiles
Size 7 Width 11 Lighten Grout 10

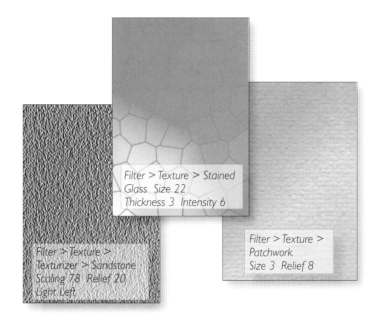

Filter > Texture > Stained Glass Size 22 Thickness 3 Intensity 6

Filter > Texture > Texturizer > Sandstone Scaling 78 Relief 20 Light Left

Filter > Texture > Patchwork Size 3 Relief 8

A helping hand

Colors generated in the computer often need some help – they are pancake flat and sometimes the filters do not work. Help improve the situation by adding Noise to your page, and then applying the filter. Some examples are shown below.

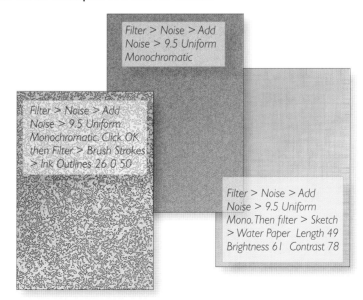

Filter > Noise > Add Noise > 9.5 Uniform Monochromatic

Filter > Noise > Add Noise > 9.5 Uniform Monochromatic. Click OK then Filter > Brush Strokes > Ink Outlines 26 0 50

Filter > Noise > Add Noise > 9.5 Uniform Mono. Then filter > Sketch > Water Paper Length 49 Brightness 61 Contrast 78

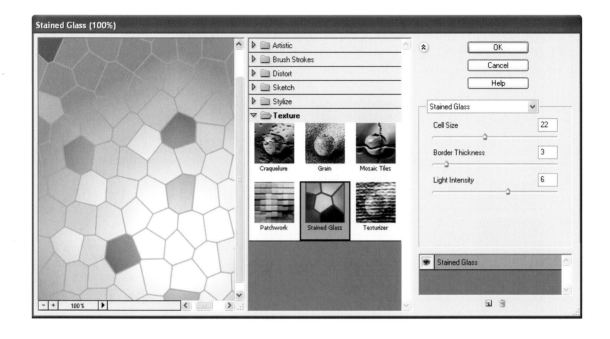

Try it Out

Keep the mouse stationary over any swatch for a couple of seconds to reveal its name.

1 Make a new file 5 x 7 inches in size and 300 pixels/inch resolution. Add a Diamond gradient. The colors used in the example are Pale Warm Brown and Pastel Blue Violet. The image is easy to make but is also available for download as Diamondgrad.jpg

2 From the menu choose Filter > Texture > Stained Glass and the large Filter Gallery dialog box shown above appears

If you apply filters and do not undo as you experiment, they will be applied on top of each other and will not look like the images shown.

3 Experiment with the settings. Take some time to look at the many options available and try and follow some of the examples shown on pages 38 and 39

4 Close the file and reward yourself for passing your first scrapbooking test!

How to Put Pictures Together

Isn't this what scrapbooking is all about? Whether it is traditional scrapbooking or digital the essential process is putting photos, papers, objects, elements, embellishments and so on together and re-arranging them into a layout that you like. In this short chapter you will see just how easy this is to do on the computer and perhaps you will start to appreciate what a great improvement digital scrapbooking can be over the traditional methods.

Covers

FourFairies.psd

TreeFairies.jpg

TwoFairies.jpg

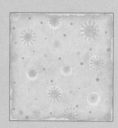

Clara's paper.jpg

Chapter Three

Copy & Paste

Clara's paper.jpg
© Clara Wallace. The full name for this commercially available paper is: "paper-green-whimsy-flowers."

Moving images together is the essence of any form of scrapbooking. In fact this chapter is probably the most important in the book. It answers many questions: How do I get this photo on that page? How do I move this embellishment to the other side of the page? Why is this paper mat on top of this photo?

There are essentially three different ways of getting images from A to B, and you will have the chance to try all three. In practice you will probably just stick with one, but it's good to know that you have a choice.

Building Pages

Hue /Saturation is explained on page 36.

1 From the menu choose File > New and make a new page with the dimensions shown here – a traditional album page

2 Open the file Clara's Paper.
This is a commercially available product (See Chapter 13). To see both files side by side select Window > Image > Tile

You could use Clara's paper as the start file if it was going to be your background and you wanted a page that is a traditional 12 inches (30 cm) square. This is not recommended. It is good practice to start off with a blank file and fit images to the size of this page. If you want to use Clara's paper with other page sizes it will have to be transformed. This is shown in later chapters.

Title black when the file is active

Title gray when the file is inactive

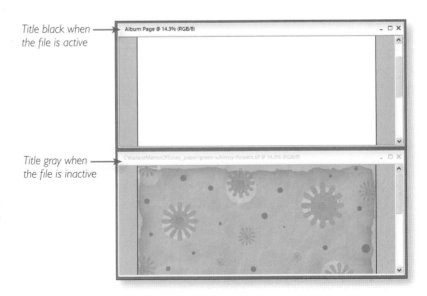

3 The problem now is how to get the paper onto the blank page. In real life you would just pick it up and put it there. The first option on the computer is the basic Copy > Paste command that you will find in all computer programs

Before you start any project make sure files are compatible in size and resolution.

4 Make sure that Clara's paper is the active file (click on the Title bar) and from the menu choose Select > All. "Marching ants" appear around the edge of the frame to show that all of the image is selected

5 From the menu choose Edit > Copy. Nothing visible happens but the image is copied to the memory of the computer

6 Close the Clara's paper file as it is no longer needed. The empty page becomes the active file. Choose Edit > Paste, and as if by magic the paper exactly covers the blank background

If nothing pasted then you did not copy properly in steps 4–5.

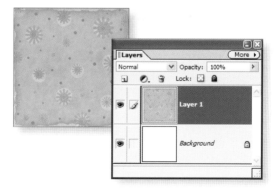

Rename the layer by double-clicking exactly on the name in the layer. The mouse cursor changes to a little hand and the text is highlighted.

7 Open the Layers palette by selecting Window > Layers and notice that a new layer has automatically been created

8 By default this is called Layer 1 as shown above. It is a good idea to change the name of this layer as shown left

9 Save the file but keep it open for the next section

Copy & Paste Again

Just to prove that it wasn't luck try the same routine again.

This Time with a Photo

TwoFairies.jpg © Lisa Thornley

1 Open the file TwoFairies.jpg and Tile to see both open files

2 Make the TwoFairies the active file. Select > All and Edit > Copy. Close the file because it is no longer needed

3 The album page is now active. Choose Edit > Paste. The photo appears in the middle of the page

Keep the Show Bounding Box in the Options bar checked.

To rename layers, see page 43.

4 Open the Layers palette to see that another layer has been created. Rename it as Two Fairies

5 Pick the Move Tool, and then click and drag the image to move it around the page. Position it at the top left of the page as shown

Copy by Dragging the Image

TreeFairies.jpg © Lisa Thornley

Dragging images from one file to another is very simple and is the method preferred by most professionals. The following technique is strongly recommended.

Drag and Drop

1 Open the file TreeFairies.jpg and choose Window > Image > Tile to see both open files

2 Make TreeFairies the active file

3 To see both files side by side select Window > Image > Tile

4 Pick the Move Tool and position it over the TreeFairies file. Click, hold and drag the image over to the album page. Release the mouse when you see a dotted rectangle and/or the cursor changes to a + sign

5 Move the image to the top right of the page and rename the layer

Sometimes dragging does not work first time. Just try again. It will happen! The cursor shape will vary according to the computer you are using.

6 Close the TreeFairies file because it is no longer needed

Copy by Dragging Layers

FourFairies.psd © Lisa Thornley

Did you read the title of this page correctly? Yes, you can drag part of an image into another. This really is a technique that the professionals use, but it is still an easy one for the beginner to master.

Pick the Correct Layer

1 Open the file FourFairies.psd and the Layer palette. To see both files side by side choose Window > Image > Tile

2 This image consists of four layers. For now it is not important to know what each does – only that it is the bottom layer, called Background, that you want to copy

3 Click on this layer to make it active. On most computers this will make it go blue

Make sure you are on the correct layer.

The active layer is blue on most computers

4 Click and hold the layer and drag it to the album page

5 The chances are that the photos are not stacked in the order that you want. This can be changed by altering the position of the layers in the palette as shown on the next page

Saving files in Photoshop PSD format preserves all the layers intact. This format is recommended for all "work in progress".

6 When all is as you want it, save the file Fairies.PSD. You will come back to this file in later chapters to make changes and add additional elements. Close the file

Layer (Stack) Order

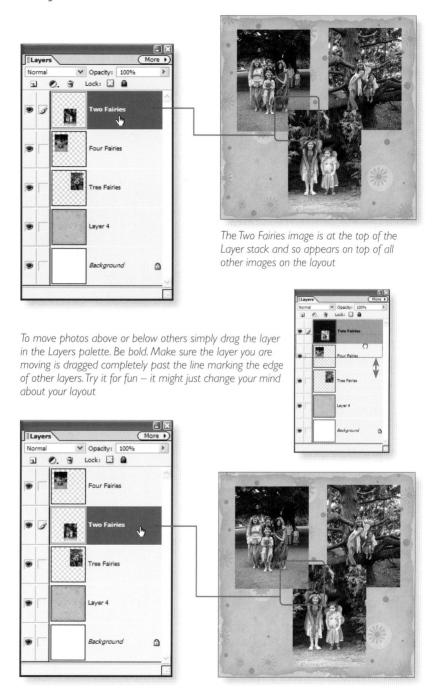

The Two Fairies image is at the top of the Layer stack and so appears on top of all other images on the layout

To move photos above or below others simply drag the layer in the Layers palette. Be bold. Make sure the layer you are moving is dragged completely past the line marking the edge of other layers. Try it for fun – it might just change your mind about your layout

The Two Fairies file is now below the Four Fairies in the stack and so its top left edge is now covered in the layout

Next Step?

If you have come this far, you will have gained some understanding of the digital process from the opening exercises. Without too much more learning, here is what you can easily achieve in the next few chapters:

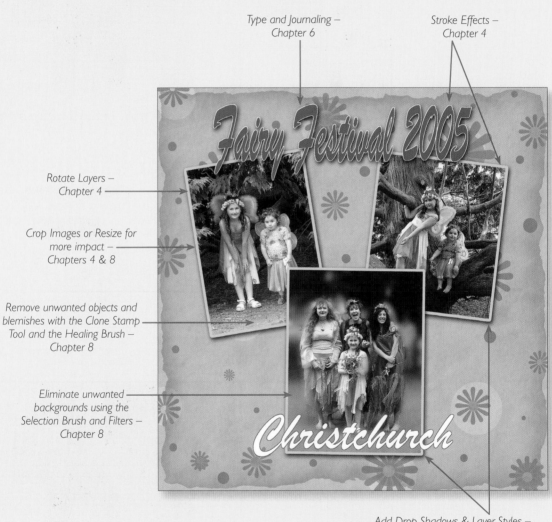

Type and Journaling –
Chapter 6

Stroke Effects –
Chapter 4

Rotate Layers –
Chapter 4

Crop Images or Resize for
more impact –
Chapters 4 & 8

Remove unwanted objects and
blemishes with the Clone Stamp
Tool and the Healing Brush –
Chapter 8

Eliminate unwanted
backgrounds using the
Selection Brush and Filters –
Chapter 8

Add Drop Shadows & Layer Styles –
Chapter 7

Flatten Layers for
a smaller file size –
Chapter 4

Frames, Borders & Mats

All images can be enhanced with lines and frames. Lines lead the eye and frames contain. Imagine a gallery where all the paintings are hung as bare canvases!

In digital scrapbooking images can be enhanced with simple lines, plain or textured mats or even virtual photo frames. Edges can be decorated with flowers, shapes, ribbons and paint effects. Frames and borders can be created in minutes, changing colors is simple and changing your mind is easy. You can even be your own picture framer!

This chapter will enhance the creative skills already gained and develop your understanding of the Selection tools. Not least, you will start to get to grips with Layers. Distressed edge effects are discussed in Chapter Five and you can try your hand at making edges with type in Chapter Six.

Covers

Victoria.jpg

Frame.jpg

Captain.jpg

Teddy.jpg

Hat.jpg

Streetwise.jpg

Dad.jpg

Faroes.jpg

Lines

A simple line around the edge of an image gives it a finished look. Those of you with a strong interest in photography will use this simple technique over and over.

Faroes.jpg © John Slater

Simple Line Border

1 Open the file Faroes.jpg

2 From the menu choose Select > All. "Marching ants" appear around the edge of the frame. You have made a "selection"

3 Make sure black is the foreground color and from the menu choose Edit > Stroke (Outline) Selection. The Stroke dialog box appears

To get rid of the selection (marching ants) use Select > Deselect. The keyboard shortcut for this is Ctrl + D.

You can change the stroke color here as well as with the foreground color

Ensure this button is checked

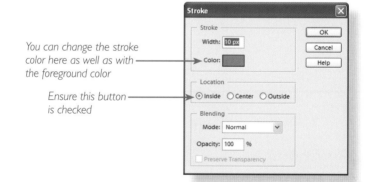

If you do not choose Inside, the stroke will either not appear or be incomplete.

4 Confirm that the color is black and all other settings are as shown above

5 Click OK and a black line appears around the outside of the photograph (shown here in close up). Keep the file open and the selection active

Eyedropper

Black is a little too gloomy so a good design idea is to use a color from the photograph. You don't have to guess this color – the Eyedropper will do this for you.

Sample the Color

1 Find the Eyedropper tool in the Toolbox

The Eyedropper has three settings. The recommended choice is 3 x 3.

Point Sample
3 by 3 Average
5 by 5 Average

2 Click on any part of the image to sample colors. The example uses a red color from one of the buildings

3 Repeat the Edit > Stroke process to change the color of the border

The drop shadow you see around the photograph is not part of the Stroke process. These shadows are created with Layer Styles and will be shown later in this chapter.

Always change file names when you want to preserve the original.

4 Save the file but use a different name, e.g. Faroes2. The original file will be used again later in this chapter

Border Command

Unlike Stroke the Border command adds a softness to the edge of the frame.

Softly Softly

The number of entries in the Undo History palette is set at 20. If this is too limiting you can change it – see page 20.

1 Open the file Faroes.jpg or if you are continuing from the previous page use the Undo History to revert to the starting image

To revert to your start position open the Undo History palette by selecting Window > Undo History and click on the top entry, Open

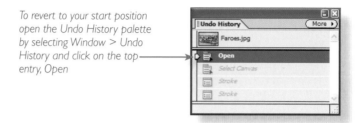

If you try and fill the border using the Paintbucket it will be messy and incomplete.

2 Make sure that the foreground color is one of the reds found in the image and from the menu choose Select > All. "Marching ants" should appear around the edge of the frame

3 From the menu choose Select > Modify > Border. In the dialog box that appears choose 85. This is rather large but will allow you to see clearly what happens with this command

4 Color the border using Edit > Fill from the menu. Use the settings shown below. Save the file and close it

A good alternative way to fill is to use the keyboard shortcut Alt + Backspace. You should try and remember this easy command.

Lines on Transparent Layers

*Sometimes it is easier to make a selection of what you do **not** want and then select the inverse to get what you do want.*

In Chapter Three you discovered how to assemble multiple files on a single background. In the last section you created lines around the edge of the image using the Stroke and Border commands. With images "floating" on layers this is not quite so simple. The trick is making the selection. All that is needed is a bit of lateral thinking.

Color the Empty Space

1 Open the file Fairies.PSD – the file you made and saved at the end of Chapter 3

If you cannot see the Layers palette, select Window > Layers.

2 Make sure the Layers palette is open and that you are on the Two Fairies layer

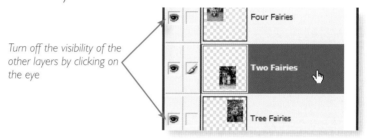

Turn off the visibility of the other layers by clicking on the eye

3 Pick the Magic Wand and select the transparent space around the image. You will see the familiar "marching ants"

Transparent areas are indicated by small gray and white squares. These do not print. You may wish to turn off the visibility of the layer. Just click on the eye. Understand that this does not delete the layer – it just makes it visible or invisible.

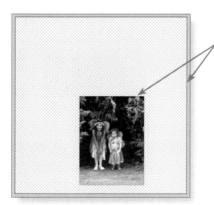

When the transparent area is selected you will see two sets of marching ants

When the image is selected there is only one

4 From the menu choose Select > Inverse to select the photograph and not the surrounding space. Easy!

5   With the Eyedropper or the Color Swatches palette pick a yellow color. The foreground color changes to show your choice

6   From the menu choose Edit > Stroke as before. This time you can stroke the transparent areas outside the image and so avoid cutting into it

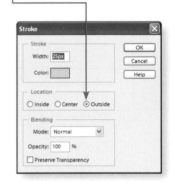

7   Repeat the process for the other two Fairy layers

8   To finish off, change the color of the paper as shown in Chapter 2. Save the file and keep it open for the next section

You need to make the paper layer active before you can change it.

Rotate Layers

Beware of the Image > Rotate command. Anything you choose from the top part of the list (shown right in pink) rotates all of the image. Choose commands from the second part (shown right in green) if you want to rotate just one element on a layer. "Friendly" layers offer you the flexibility to change exactly what you want to.

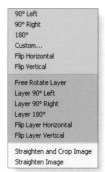

The active layer on most computers is colored blue.

Make a Little Turn

1 The Fairies.PSD file you changed in the previous exercise should still be open

2 Make sure the Layers palette is open and that the "Four Fairies" layer is active

The Free Rotate command is not available if your image does not have layers.

3 From the menu choose Image > Rotate > Free Rotate Layer. A box appears around the photo

Move your mouse outside the box to rotate

Cancel or Commit to changes

4 Put your mouse OUTSIDE the box and the cursor will change to a two-headed bent arrow. Simply move the mouse and the image rotates

You can also cancel by pressing the Esc (escape) key on the keyboard.

5 To accept the changes either press the Enter key on the keyboard or the Commit button in the Options bar

Resize Layers

Resize works in a very similar way to Rotate. Again you should not be confused by Image > Resize > Image Size, which will change the size of the whole image.

Bigger or Smaller

Drag from the corners and hold down the Shift key to keep the perspective correct. If you don't, the image may be distorted.

1 Make the Tree Fairies layer active

2 From the menu choose Image > Resize > Scale.
A box appears around the photo

Unusual keyboard keys are shown on page 16.

Handles

Cancel or Commit to changes

Drag from the corners

3 Drag one of the handles to adjust the size

The keyboard shortcut to save the file is Ctrl + S.

4 Accept or cancel the changes with the buttons in the Options bar or the Enter / Escape (Esc) keys

5 Save the file but keep it open for the next section

Shadows for a 3D Effect

You don't have to make your digital layouts look like conventional pages, but if you want to do this then you need to be aware of shadows. Just about everything in real life has a shadow and with traditional albums the fact that objects are piled on top of each other means they invariably create their own shadows – have a close look and see.

A good rule for digital layouts is to put shadows on all elements except journaling text. Journaling is supposed to be part of the page (the ink sinks into the paper) rather than floating on top, so it doesn't usually need a shadow.

Use gentle, subtle shadows to give the appearance of elements stuck to the page and larger shadows for elements like ribbons, tags or buttons that would clearly be on top of the page. As well as using shadows, you can enhance the 3D illusion with bevels and embossing, which will be demonstrated in later chapters.

If you can't see the Styles & Effects palette, check the Styles & Effects option on the Window menu.

Pop Out of the Page

1   The Tree Fairies layer should still be active

2   Open the Styles and Effects palette, which is usually located to the right of your workspace. Adjust the two drop-down boxes to Layer Styles and Drop Shadows. Click on one of the choices

You may find it easier to see the shadow effect if you turn off the visibility of some of the layers.

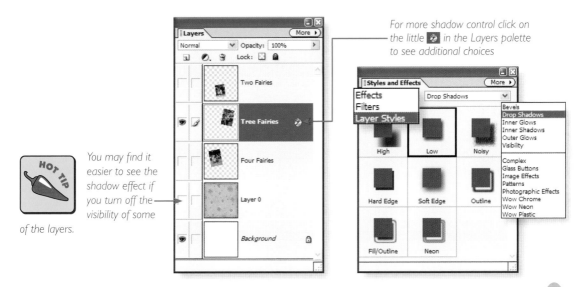

For more shadow control click on the little [image] in the Layers palette to see additional choices

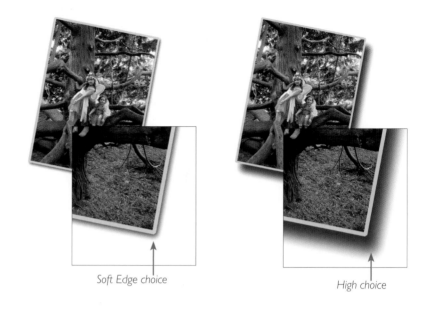

Soft Edge choice

High choice

More Control

1 The choices available should suit most purposes but if you need a little more finesse there is an option. Click on the little ⧉ in the active layer to show the Style Settings dialog

2 Experiment to see what the box does. Click OK

3 Save and close the file

9780760778609
Digital scrapbooking kit

Canvas & Canvas Size

Dad.jpg © Sue Francis

The Border command and to some extent the Stroke command have the disadvantage of cutting into the image. This is fine if there is nothing important at the edges of the photo. Wouldn't it be nice, however, if you could add some extra space around your image so this would not happen? Well, you can, and it's not that difficult with the Canvas Size command. You can also use this technique to create mats for journaling.

How Big is this Photo?

The Canvas Size command allows you to add space around an image. You control where the extra space appears with the Anchor Box.

1 Open the file Dad.jpg and make a note of the Image size using Image > Resize > Image Size

2 Check the Canvas Size using Image > Resize > Canvas Size. You will find that they are the same – for the time being!

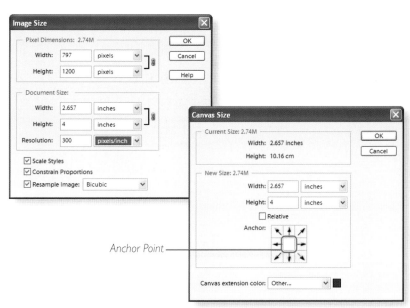

Anchor Point —

3 Add some space around the image. Increase the width and height by one inch, leave the Anchor box with the central square checked and click OK. The result is shown at the top of the next page

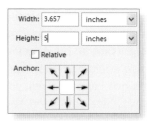

The Anchor Box positioned in the middle means that the original image appears in the middle of the new canvas

4 Notice how the extra space is even all around the image. Undo this and experiment with different settings in the size boxes and different anchor positions as shown below

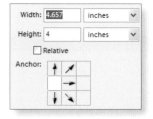

The new canvas will be the background color unless you make a choice from the drop-down list.

The Anchor Box positioned left means that the original image remains on the left side of the new canvas

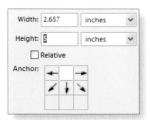

The Anchor Box positioned top means that the original image remains at the top of the new canvas

5 Save and close the file

Multi-Line Borders

The simple Canvas Size command can be enhanced to create sophisticated multi-line borders. Thick, thin, different colors? Plain or textured, flat or beveled? You choose. Here's how.

Little Mac?

Mac.jpg © Jackie Tyne

1 Open the file Mac.jpg. You will make a four-line border using two colors from the photo. Set the two colors wanted with the Eyedropper. Pick a pale blue color from the bed linen. Swap the Toolbox colors and pick a buff color from Mac's shirt

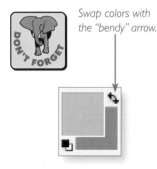

Swap colors with the "bendy" arrow.

2 In the Canvas Size dialog box change the measurements to "pixels" and add just 10 pixels

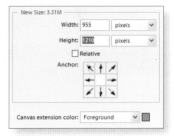

3 Swap the foreground color and increase the Canvas Size evenly by 30 pixels

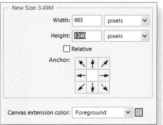

Save the chosen colors to the Swatches palette as shown on page 28.

4 Swap the colors again and increase the Canvas Size by 15 pixels

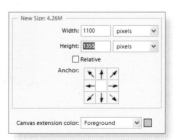

5 Swap the colors again and increase the Canvas Size by 100 pixels

6 The finished image is shown top left on the next page

What Next?

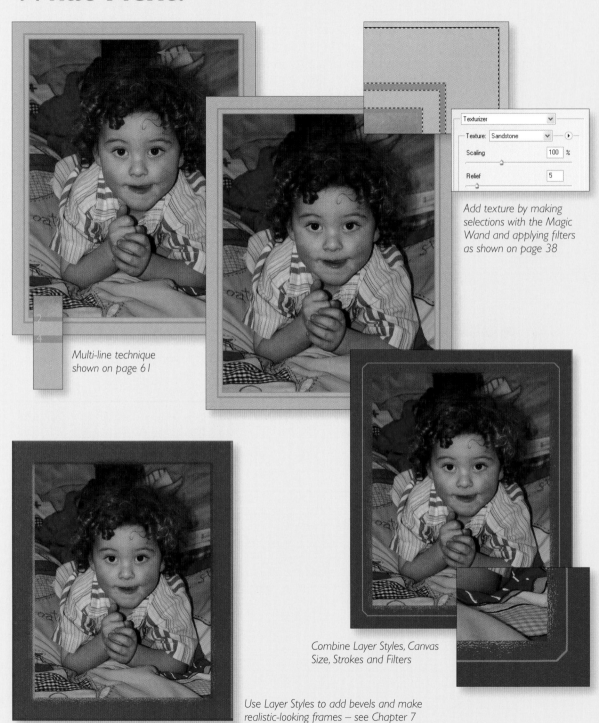

Multi-line technique
shown on page 61

Add texture by making
selections with the Magic
Wand and applying filters
as shown on page 38

Combine Layer Styles, Canvas
Size, Strokes and Filters

Use Layer Styles to add bevels and make
realistic-looking frames – see Chapter 7

An Old-Fashioned Vignette

Victoria.jpg

Popular in Victorian times and on many a mantelpiece are images framed with a soft edge. These are commonly oval shaped and have ornate frames. Both effects are easy to achieve on the computer.

Little Softy

1 Open the file Victoria.jpg. This file has already been hand colored

2 Select the Elliptical Marquee tool from the Toolbox. Remember it may be hiding behind another tool – if so, click and hold on the visible tool to reveal those beneath

The Elliptical Marquee tool is used to make circular or elliptical selections. Simply drag to make the shape. If this is not exactly as you wish, click outside the selection and it will disappear.

3 Drag the mouse to create a circular shape over the head. The marching ants indicate that you have a selection and you should now know that any action you now take will affect only the selected area. If you don't like the selection you have made simply click outside the marching ants, or choose Select > Deselect, and they disappear. Then try again

4 For this exercise you want to change the area outside the selection so choose Select > Inverse

5 Make sure white is the foreground color and fill the selected area. You should end up with something similar to this:

When using the Elliptical Marquee tool it is very difficult, if not impossible, to draw a perfect circle freehand. Instead, press and hold down the Shift key while dragging the selection. For a perfect square, do the same with the Rectangular Marquee tool.

Hard edge

If you want a softer edge, similar to the vignettes popular with Victorian photographers, you will need to soften or feather the selection.

1 Revert back to your starting point. There are several ways to do this. In this instance use File > Revert

2 Make your selection again and then select the inverse

3 Now choose Select > Feather. The Feather Selection box appears. Set the value to 25 pixels, which will give noticeable softness

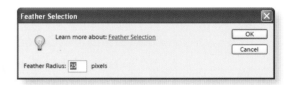

Revert back again and try different values in the Feather Selection box. Try to get a feel for what is happening. Note that the effect will be influenced by the resolution of the image. With high resolution images larger feather values are needed to achieve any desired effect.

4 Click OK. You will not see anything until you fill the selection, using Edit > Fill Layer > Foreground Color. Then... hey presto Victoriana!

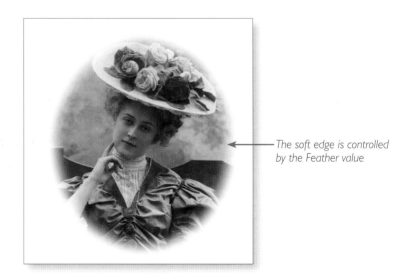

The soft edge is controlled by the Feather value

Cookie Cutter

Cut out your pictures to just about any shape you could imagine – a diamond, an elephant, a flower. You can do this in most image editing software and it really is very easy in Photoshop Elements. The effect is very similar to die cuts in traditional scrapbooking but with the advantage that shapes can be altered in size and distorted at the click of a button. The choice is simply amazing!

Streetwise.jpg © John Slater

SuperStar

1 Open the file Streetwise.jpg

2 Find the Cookie Cutter tool and look at the shapes available

3 Pick the Heart Card shape and drag over the image. Control the overall shape by dragging the handles. When you let go, the image is cut out of its background in the shape of the heart

Don't worry if you don't get the shape perfect first time – it can be adjusted. Just drag the handles.

4 To use the file now and preserve the cutout shape, drag it onto another file. To keep the cutout shape for later use save in either Photoshop PSD or PNG format

If you close or flatten the file at this stage, the shape will have a white background. To use the cutout shape, the file needs to be dragged onto another image. To preserve as a shape on a transparent background save in Photoshop PSD format.

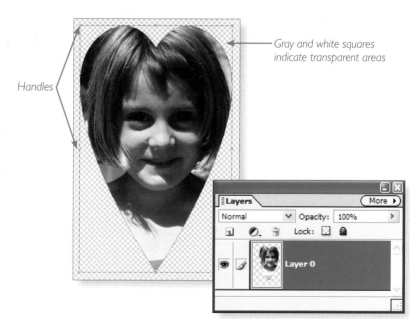

Gray and white squares indicate transparent areas

Handles

Cookie Cutter Options

 Shape: Shape Options: ▼ Feather: 0 px ☐ Crop

 To customize or add additional shapes

Text Only
✓ Small Thumbnail
Large Thumbnail
Small List
Large List

✓ All Elements Shapes
Animals
Animals2
Arrows
Banners and Awards
Characters
Crop Shapes
Default
Dressup
Face
Flowers
Foliage and Trees
Food
Frames
Fruit
Music
Nature
Objects
Ornaments
Shapes
Signs

10-Point Star with additional double stroke

Crop Shape 13

Flower 28

Heart Card

Type as a Frame

Teddy.jpg
Original © Gem Fonts

Hat.jpg © John Slater

You will learn lots more interesting techniques with type in Chapter 6. For now you will see how easy it is to use wonderful typefaces available free on the internet as frames for your photos.

Bearly Difficult?

1 Open the files Teddy.jpg and Hat.jpg. The Teddy image was originally part of a font. (See Chapter 13 for sources of unusual fonts)

2 To arrange the images on the page use Window > Images >Tile

3 Make sure that the Hat file is active and then choose Select > All

4 From the menu select Edit > Copy. This copies the selected area to the memory of the computer. Close the Hat file because it is no longer needed

5 The Teddy file is now active. Pick the Magic Wand and select the area inside the heart

6 From the menu choose Edit > Paste Into Selection. Miraculously the hat image appears inside the heart – but maybe the wrong part of the photo is showing. Pick the Move Tool and drag the photo to where you want it. Spooky!

To get rid of the selection (marching ants) use Select > Deselect.
The keyboard shortcut for this is Ctrl + D.

Make sure you use Paste Into Selection and not just Paste.

But what if you want to see more of the picture?

Big Head?

1 Zoom out so that you can see all of the image and lots of the desktop (usually colored gray)

When you transform, hold down the Shift key to maintain correct perspective.

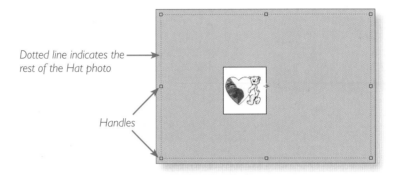

Dotted line indicates the rest of the Hat photo

Handles

2 You will see a faint dotted line. This indicates the rest of the Hat picture that you cannot see

3 From the menu choose Image > Transform > Free Transform and drag from the corner handles to adjust the size

Once you have deselected you cannot change your mind unless you use the Undo History palette. All entries in this palette are eliminated once files are closed or when the computer is turned off.

4 When you are happy with the results, press the Enter key to accept the changes. Save the file as BearHeart.tif and close

Photoshop Users Take Note

There is a fundamental difference between the workings of Photoshop and Photoshop Elements when pasting images together.

The Extra Layer

If you open the Layers palette using Window > Layers and repeat the last exercise you will see that in Photoshop Elements there is only one layer, called Background, throughout the whole process.

Photoshop Elements maintains a single layer throughout the process

If you are a Photoshop user, you will find that the Edit > Paste Into command automatically creates a second layer, which by default is called Layer 1. This layer will stay until you either remove it or flatten the file. Leaving the layer intact means that you can come back and change the layer at any time you wish – your flexibility is not compromised.

Photoshop automatically creates a second layer and a Layer Mask to enhance the editing flexibility

Photoshop Elements users have to be slightly more careful because once you close the file there is no easy way of going back. You may end up doing the work again. That said, there will be no difference in the finished results if you use either program properly.

Use a Real Photo Frame

Frame.jpg © John Slater

Now that you have grasped the idea of adding borders and putting images into shapes, why not become your own picture framer? The gold frame used in this example was simply scanned, but there are lots of great frames freely available on the internet.

Looking Good in Gold?

Captain.jpg © John Slater

1 Open the files Frame.jpg and Captain.jpg

2 To arrange the images on the page use Window > Images >Tile

3 Look at the two images. The frame is portrait shaped; the photo is landscape shaped. To correct this make sure that the frame is the active file and from the menu choose Image > Rotate 90° Left

Embossed frame available for free download from www.cottagearts.net

4 Make the Captain file active and from the menu choose Select > All. Follow this with Edit > Copy. Close the Captain file because it is no longer needed

5 Select the inside of the frame with the Magic Wand and use Edit > Paste Into Selection

6 Use the Move Tool and just drag the inner image to where you want it. Then choose Image > Transform > Free Transform to scale and fit the frame correctly. Accept the changes.

Remember when you copy anything it will go into the memory of the computer and will stay there until something else is copied or the computer is turned off.

Drag handle to resize

Custom Shapes

Having made all this exciting progress, now it's easy to make a simple mat that you will use over and over again. The Shape tools allow you to create just about any shape you can think of, and Custom Shapes allow you to create complex objects at the click of a button. Get started here and gain more experience and sophistication in later chapters.

Shape Layers can be merged together to create complex shapes. You will do this when making tags on page 125.

Simple Shapes – Easy Mats

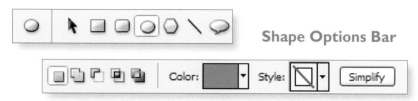

Shape Options Bar

1 Make a new file with the mini-album dimensions shown below

When you drag the shape hold down the Shift key to keep perfect squares or perfect circles.

2 Pick the Rounded Rectangle Shape tool, choose a purple color and drag a rectangle on the empty canvas. Control the roundness of the corners with the Radius setting in the Options bar

3 Open the Layers palette and see that the shape appears on its own layer. Rename the layer as Purple Mat

You will get a warning asking if you want to Simplify the layer. You must do so if you want to add a texture.

4 Add some texture using the Filters you already know (see page 38). The example below used Texture > Texturizer > Canvas, followed by Artistic > Colored Pencil

5 Open the file Captain.jpg and drag it onto the mat

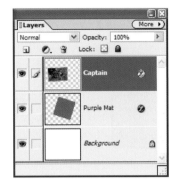

6 Add a thick stroke around the image and reposition both elements. Add a drop shadow for the final effect

7 Squash the layers together with Layer > Flatten > Image. Save the file and close it

Make your own Papers

Papers form the base of virtually all scrapbooking projects. There are so many possibilities it would be easy to write a book solely on making papers. This chapter helps you discover the processes behind some of the concepts. With just a few basics you should be able to produce papers that are unique. Textures, stripes, checks, ginghams and florals are all within your reach. You will also see how easy it is to recreate the torn paper edges so common in traditional scrapbooking. Techniques for papers covered with type are shown in Chapter Six.

Covers

Chapter Five

Nik.jpg   Tiger.jpg   Kalahari.jpg

Eazy-Peazy Papers

Chapter Two gave some basics for coloring in and adding texture. This chapter adds sophistication, and once you understand the concepts there are millions of options for you to play with. You could stay on this chapter for hours! You will start with a couple of really easy techniques.

More Filter Effects

In this book Resolution will always be in pixels/inch not pixels/cm. If you make a mistake with this the best solution is to close the file you are working on and start again.

1 Make a new page. Shown here is the traditional square album page

2 Pick new foreground and background colors. The colors used in this exercise are shown below

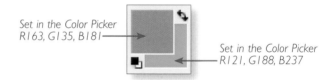

Set in the Color Picker R163, G135, B181

Set in the Color Picker R121, G188, B237

If your computer is not very powerful, it may run slowly when applying filters. Unless you buy extra memory (RAM) you will have to be patient!

3 From the menu choose Layer > New > Layer and give this new layer a name. You will understand why you need this extra layer shortly

4 From the menu choose Filter > Render > Clouds. For some projects this page may already be finished. If you find the effect a little too strong and want a more subtle pastel effect simply change the Opacity in the Layers palette

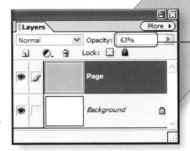

Reduce the Opacity to give the page a more pastel appearance. You cannot do this if there is only a single Background layer

Build a library of pages by saving the files you like. Remember to use a different file name for each page.

5 For the more adventurous, apply another filter on top of the existing Clouds effect. It only takes seconds and the results can be amazing. Save the best ones

The subtlety of the changes shown here will be more apparent on the computer monitor than on the printed page.

Clouds filter followed by Filter > Render > Fibers

Clouds followed by Filter > Render > Fibers and on top of this Filter > Distort > Ocean Ripple

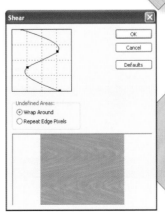

Clouds filter followed by Filter > Distort > Shear. Click on the vertical line and drag to the side

Super Eazy Noizy Gradient Papers

Great name! At the start of this book you made simple pages using gradients. Now it's time to explore and find the good stuff. Hidden deep is a secret especially for digital scrappers – the Noise Gradient.

More Noise Equals More Colors

1 Make a new page. The examples shown were created on a traditional square album page

2 Make a new layer and name it Green–White

3 Set the foreground and background colors to green and white as shown here

4 Pick the Gradient tool in the Toolbox. Click the Edit button in the Options bar to reveal the Gradient Editor

Photoshop users have to click inside the gradient preview to get the Editor. There is no Edit button.

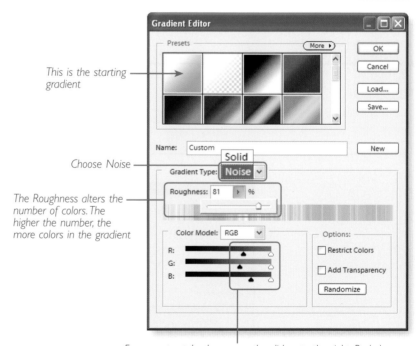

This is the starting gradient

Choose Noise

The Roughness alters the number of colors. The higher the number, the more colors in the gradient

For more pastel colors move the sliders to the right. Red changes the number of cyans, green affects the number of magentas and pinks, and blue the number and intensity of yellows

5 Change the Gradient Type to Noise, increase the Roughness value, and restrict the RGB sliders as shown opposite

6 Using the Linear gradient drag a diagonal line from corner to corner to get a page looking something like this:

Do not expect to get exactly the same colors as shown here. While you should get something similar there are too many variables to expect a perfect match.

7 Duplicate the layer and rotate it by 90°. The image and your Layers palette should look like this:

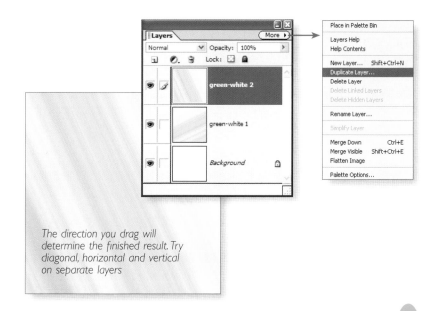

The direction you drag will determine the finished result. Try diagonal, horizontal and vertical on separate layers

Blending & Opacity

Layers can be opaque, translucent or transparent. The blending modes in the Layers palette tell a layer how to react with the pixels in the layer beneath. In combination, these provide new avenues and untold opportunities for the digital scrapbooker, especially those making their own papers.

Beautiful Blends

1 At the top of the Layers palette there is a choice of blending modes and Opacity. Change the blend mode to Multiply. The two layers are blended together

2 If the effect is too strong reduce the Opacity of one or both layers until you get a blend that you like

3 Save the file in Photoshop PSD format to preserve the layers for future experiments

If your mouse has a scroll wheel you can quickly scroll through the blending list and save a lot of repetitive clicking.

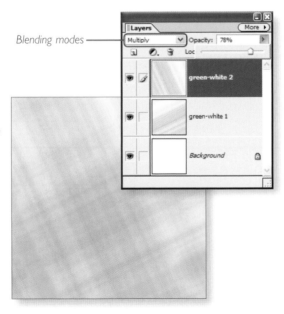

Blending modes

Try different blending modes. Depending upon the image, some modes will have a strong effect while others have little effect. Most users will be content to experiment and accept the amazing results. If you want to know what is happening technically, consult the Help files in the software.

Normal
Dissolve

Darken
Multiply
Color Burn
Linear Burn

Lighten
Screen
Color Dodge
Linear Dodge

Overlay
Soft Light
Hard Light
Vivid Light
Linear Light
Pin Light
Hard Mix

Difference
Exclusion

Hue
Saturation
Color
Luminosity

Beautiful Variations

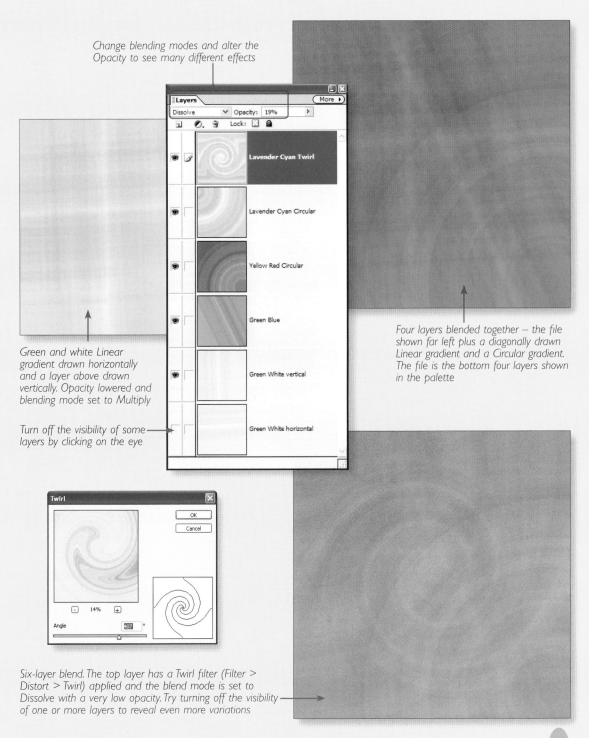

Change blending modes and alter the Opacity to see many different effects

Green and white Linear gradient drawn horizontally and a layer above drawn vertically. Opacity lowered and blending mode set to Multiply

Turn off the visibility of some layers by clicking on the eye

Lavender Cyan Twirl

Lavender Cyan Circular

Yellow Red Circular

Green Blue

Green White vertical

Green White horizontal

Four layers blended together – the file shown far left plus a diagonally drawn Linear gradient and a Circular gradient. The file is the bottom four layers shown in the palette

Six-layer blend. The top layer has a Twirl filter (Filter > Distort > Twirl) applied and the blend mode is set to Dissolve with a very low opacity. Try turning off the visibility of one or more layers to reveal even more variations

Striped Pages

Just as easy are pages containing stripes. You will start to input some of your own ideas and take control. The computer will do what you ask. In the process you will master the Rectangular Marquee Selection tool.

Pyjamas?

Whatever page size you choose set the Resolution to 300 pixels/ inch if you want to print it out at photographic quality.

1 Make a new page. This example uses the traditional square album page

2 Open the Swatches palette and add your chosen colors. The example uses six pastels

Adding colors to the bottom of the Swatches palette is described on page 28. Doing this helps you quickly locate a specific color and is strongly recommended.

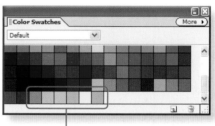

Colors chosen for this exercise

3 Make a new layer by using Layer > New > Layer and call it "Pink Base". Fill this layer with a pink color (Pastel Magenta)

Fill using the Paintbucket or the shortcut keys Alt/Option plus Backspace.

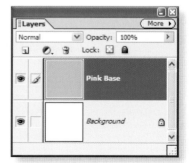

The Rectangular Marquee tool is used to make square or rectangular selections. Simply drag to make the shape. If this is not exactly as you wish, click outside the selection and it will disappear.

4 Pick the Rectangular Marquee tool and drag a selection from top left to the bottom of the page as shown. Fill with pastel yellow

This is your first stripe. Adjust the width of the stripe as you drag

Make sure you drag from the very top to the very bottom of the page

5 Repeat this several times. Each time alter the width of the selection and fill with a different color. Keep the selections to one half of the page as shown

You can also use Shapes to draw the stripes and the color will fill automatically. Each stripe will appear on its own layer – if you are not careful this can be confusing.

6 When the stripes cover about half of the page save some time. Duplicate the layer and rotate it by using Layer > Duplicate Layer followed by Image > Rotate Layer > 180°. The Layers palette should look as shown here.

Photoshop users can rotate the layer by using Edit > Free Transform.

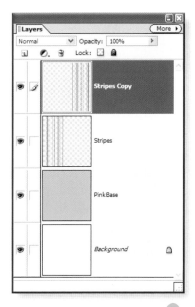

7 Click on the More button at the top of the palette and choose Merge Down. The two stripes layers are merged into one. Adjust the Opacity and blend mode as previously shown

Make sure you are on the correct layer before you Merge Down. In this case you should be on the rotated copy layer.

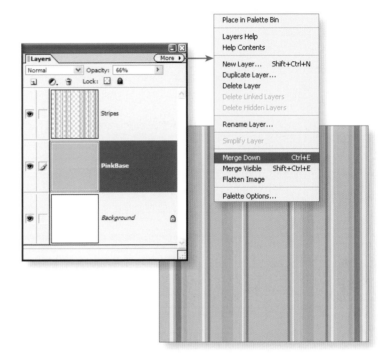

8 Make the Pink Base layer active and add some Noise or similar texture. Merge or Flatten as you wish. Save the file and close

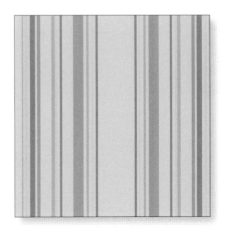

Yellow Check

As a natural progression from stripes it is easy to create a criss-cross check pattern. If you take care with the setting up then the ease with which you create this is bound to impress. You will set the Rectangular Marquee to automatically draw a fixed sized rectangle the size of each stripe.

In Photoshop, guides make the placement of selections much easier.

Table Cloth

1 Make a new page. This example uses the traditional twelve inch square album page

Set the Rulers to any unit of measurement you like in Preferences. This example uses inches.

2 From the menu choose View > Rulers. Make sure the Rulers are set in inches by using Edit > Preferences > Units & Rulers

3 Pick the Rectangular Marquee tool and look at the Options bar. Choose Fixed Size and enter the settings shown below

4 Position the mouse in the top left corner of the page at the 0–0 position as shown below

An alternative to making your own papers is to buy on the internet. The paper below is plaid-citrus from www. matterofscrap.com.

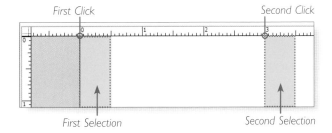

First Click   Second Click

First Selection   Second Selection

5 Click on the blank page and a selection magically appears. Fill it with yellow

6 Move the mouse to the 3 inch position and click again. Another rectangle appears. Fill it with yellow

7 Continue across the page at 2½-inch intervals. You will end with a set of horizontal stripes like this:

Stripes to Check

1 When the layer is complete, duplicate it and rotate the copy 90° by using Layer > Duplicate Layer, followed by Image > Rotate > Rotate Layer 90°

2 Change the blending mode to Multiply and reduce the Opacity to create the finished paper

3 Flatten the image by using Layer > Flatten Image and save it

Change Blending Mode

Reduce Opacity

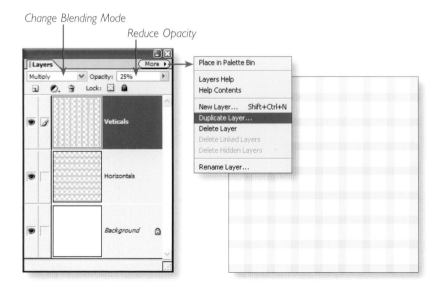

RedButton.psd

What Next?

Once you have the basic fabric you can make all sorts of changes. Just remember to save any images you want to keep with different file names. One idea is to add buttons.

Button it

When you make a duplicate you will not see any change in the image until the duplicate layer is repositioned with the Move tool.

1 Open the file RedButton.psd and drag it onto the check paper. Position it at the intersection of the stripes

2 Duplicate the button layer and move the duplicate to a new position. If you want, change the color using the Hue/Saturation command. Repeat as many times as you wish

3 Flatten the layers. Save the file and close it

The Button.psd file was made entirely from scratch in Photoshop Elements. Many others are available for free download. The one shown below is from www.escrappers.com. The original file is button.psd. Open the Layers palette and you will have a choice of buttons simply by changing the visibility of the layers. You will also get a good idea on how you can make your own buttons.

Duplicate the button layer and change the color using Hue/Saturation

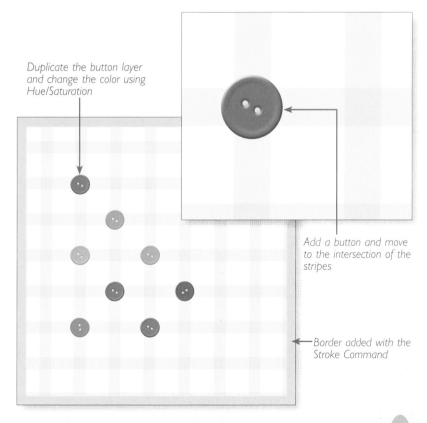

Add a button and move to the intersection of the stripes

Border added with the Stroke Command

Patterns

Nik.jpg © Aoraki Team

Patterns appear everywhere – on fabrics, as wallpaper or on the background of web pages. Although they are fun to create don't be fooled into thinking that Photoshop Elements has magical powers in this area – because it hasn't! Simple patterns are easy; complex patterns are difficult. They require a great deal of planning and understanding. The exercises here are just a "taster" – just to get you thinking about the great possibilities the program offers. Master this chapter and you are well on the way to being a good digital scrapbooker!

Multi me

1 You can make a simple tiled pattern out of anything. To prove this open the file Nik.jpg

2 Pick the Rectangular Marquee tool and draw a selection over Nik's face. Any rectangular shape will work

All patterns are based upon a rectangular selection. It is this area that becomes the individual "tile" in the pattern

3 From the menu choose Edit > Define pattern from Selection. When prompted give the new pattern a name

4 Make a blank file to accept the new pattern. This example uses a traditional twelve inch square page

5 Then use Edit > Fill > Pattern. Find the NikFace pattern from the drop-down box and you will end up with something like this:

The pattern effect will depend upon the size and resolution of the blank file.

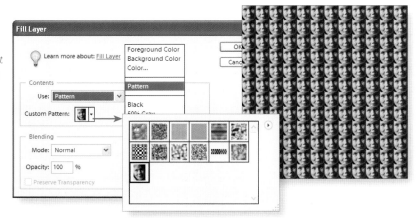

6 If you are feeling adventurous turn the background into something more artistic using filters. Save and close the file

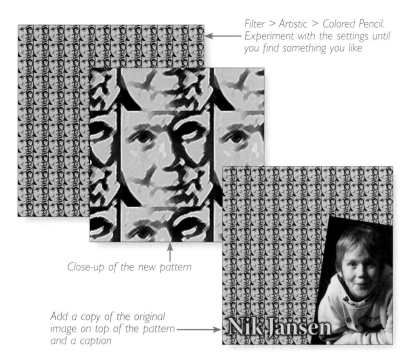

Filter > Artistic > Colored Pencil. Experiment with the settings until you find something you like

Close-up of the new pattern

Add a copy of the original image on top of the pattern and a caption

Blended Patterns

Flower.psd

Now that you realize how easy and how much fun it is to make a simple tiled pattern, repeat the process but put the pattern onto a new layer. This way you are able to blend and add textures to the pattern as you did in previous exercises.

Floral Display

1 Open the file Flower.psd and the Layers palette. This is simply a die cut from a traditional scrapbooker's cutter on a black background

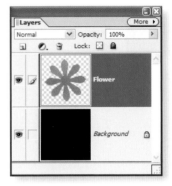

2 Ensure the Flower layer is active. Select All and define a new pattern called "Flower"

3 Make a new file. Add a "Base" layer and color it blue

4 Make another new layer and call it Pattern. Fill the layer with the flower pattern. Your image will look something like this:

Close-up of the new pattern. Simple patterns are always "tiled" in appearance

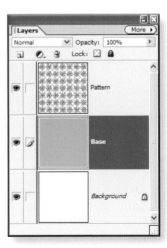

5 By altering blending modes and opacity and by adding filters a vast array of pages can be created from the single pattern

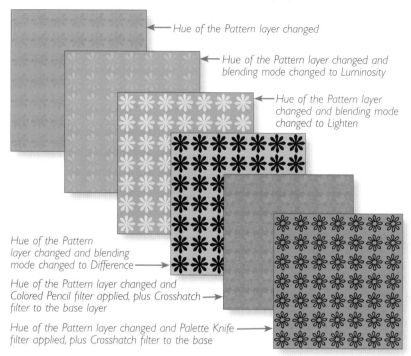

← Hue of the Pattern layer changed

← Hue of the Pattern layer changed and blending mode changed to Luminosity

← Hue of the Pattern layer changed and blending mode changed to Lighten

Hue of the Pattern layer changed and blending mode changed to Difference →

Hue of the Pattern layer changed and Colored Pencil filter applied, plus Crosshatch filter to the base layer →

Hue of the Pattern layer changed and Palette Knife filter applied, plus Crosshatch filter to the base →

An alternative to making your own papers is to buy on the internet. The paper below is pattern-distress1 from www.matterofscrap.com.

Offset Patterns

Patterns that are offset or less "tiled" in appearance just need a different starting selection. Select one flower and copy it to a blank layer or file. Add a second flower and position it diagonally. Make a new selection and define the new pattern. Have a go!

Close-up of the new offset pattern

Photo Page

Tiger.jpg © Janine Burgess

Kalahari.jpg © Janine Burgess

A collection of photographs makes the perfect base for a travel project, especially if the background is muted or monotone. You already know how to put images on a page and resize them. This exercise shows how to blend images together and also suggests alternative ways of using these pages.

South Africa

1. Make a new page. This example uses the traditional square album page. Add a new base layer and fill with color. The example shows a sandy color sampled from the Tiger image, with gentle Burlap texture added as shown on page 40

2. Open all the images you need and drag them onto the blank file. In the example there were fifteen images but for this exercise you only need two files, Tiger.jpg and Kalahari.jpg

3. Name all layers for easy identification; move and resize them to suit. It may help if the images are overlapped

Only two of the images shown for this project are available on the website. Use your own images to create a truly personal paper.

Keep all the images together in a specific folder.

Sample colors with the Eyedropper tool.

← *Real layout example*

Simple layout for the exercise

If you use lots of images the file size will be very large and you should expect your computer to be slow, especially when applying filters.

This page already looks great but make it even more impressive by blending the different images together. This is easy because each image is on its own layer. The process is the same regardless of the number of images you have, and works best when one layer overlaps the layer beneath.

Blend

1 Make sure the Tiger layer is at the top of the Layers stack

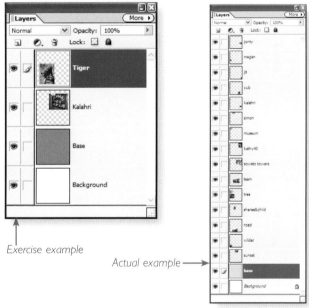

Exercise example

Actual example →

Eraser Options Bar

2 Pick the Eraser Tool and set the Brush Size at 95 px (pixels) and 100% Opacity

3 Brush along the top edge of the Tiger image and see the edge disappear

The blending process is more flexible and easier if your software has Layer Masks, as found in all versions of Photoshop (see page 69).

4 Choose Edit > Undo. You do not need such a sharp erase; a partial erase or blend would look better. Change the Opacity to 25% and repeat the eraser stroke. Only part of the Tiger image is removed

5 Continue with the eraser using a strong eraser (high Opacity) at the edges and a gentle eraser (low Opacity) away from the edges. With care you should be able to create a blend between the two layers

Change the Opacity to give more or less erasure and so create a blend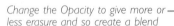

Calm down or Enhance?

By itself this could be the finished background and only a few words are needed to finish the layout.

If you want a more artistic approach one of the numerous filters can be applied to give a hand-painted effect.

If your layout needs more words, calm the busy background by one of the options shown opposite.

More Choice

To get the overall blue color use Image > Enhance > Adjust Color > Adjust Hue/Saturation. Check the Colorize button and use settings similar to Hue 15, Saturation 20 and Lightness +5

To get the watermark effect simply increase the Lightness value in the Hue/Saturation dialog

Frustrated artist? Try filters for a painted effect. Here: Artistic > Colored Pencil, Pencil Width 6, Stroke Pressure 4, Paper Brightness 47

Budding Van Gogh? Try different filters. Here: Artistic > Watercolor, Brush Detail 8, Shadow Intensity 0, Texture 2

If you want to add journaling why not replace one of the photos with a mat and type on top?

The New Zealand Group Study Exchange team's South African travel experience. Clockwise from left: Johannesburg's imposing Apartheid Museum; team member Simon Mapp; a Mabalingwe sunset; team member Kathryn Hishon; a lone tree at a Mabalingwe watering hole; team member Sheree Mortimer - always popular with the children; Soweto's trademark towers; team member Megan Grindlay; team leader Jonathon Usher; a truly African luxury lodge banner; the welcoming buffalo; the team practicing African culture immersion; tiger cub antics; team member Janine Burgess.

Painted Pages

At a basic level, the Brush tool works like a traditional paintbrush that you might use to decorate your house. Brushes can be different sizes and have hard or soft edges. The Brush tool, Eraser, Clone Stamp, Healing Brush, Burn and Dodge tools all work with brushes and behave similarly at this basic level. Digital brushes have magical qualities. They can be shaped; they can be textured. More creatively, you can control how each stroke fades, alters in size and changes color as the paint is applied.

On this page you will have fun discovering how you can paint flat pages. Elsewhere brushes are used for enhancement and effect. There is a great deal about brushes that is not said here. You are urged to experiment and gain experience of this amazing and universal tool.

Monet? Not quite!

To follow this exercise exactly use the Color Picker to set exact colors. The Green is: R42, G199, B93. Orange is: R246, G131, B18. Red is: R250, B6, G46.

1. Make a new file. This demonstration uses a square mini album page. Make a new "Base" layer and color it green. Add gentle texture

2. Make a new blank layer and call it Maple Leaves. Pick the Brush tool and find the Scattered Maple Leaves brush. Set the Options bar as shown opposite

3. Click on More Options and set the dynamic options as shown

4. Click and drag across the top of the page to "paint" with multi-colored maple leaves. Continue around the rest of the page

Keep the paint on a separate layer. This will allow you to add layer styles and effects.

5. Increase the Brush Size to 250 and Spacing to 200 and repeat the painting process

Brush Tool Options

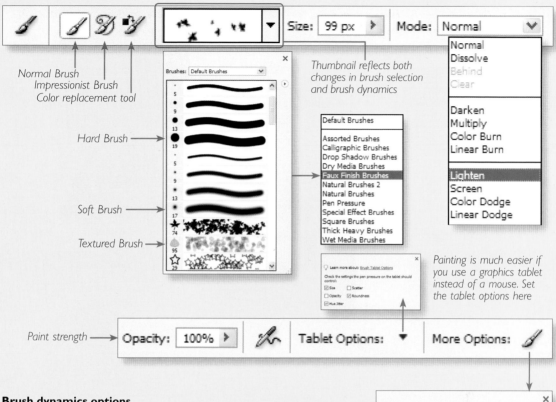

Normal Brush
Impressionist Brush
Color replacement tool

Thumbnail reflects both
changes in brush selection
and brush dynamics

Hard Brush

Soft Brush

Textured Brush

Painting is much easier if
you use a graphics tablet
instead of a mouse. Set
the tablet options here

Paint strength → Opacity: 100% ▸   Tablet Options: ▾   More Options:

Brush dynamics options

*Dynamics change the characteristics of a brush over
the course of a brush stroke. There are several controls:*

Spacing. *Controls the distance between individual brush marks
in a stroke. For scrapbookers, this option is useful for
creating dotted lines and simulating needle stitching.*

Fade. *Sets the number of steps until the paint stroke fades
to nothing. A low value makes the paint
stroke fade quickly. Use a high value for
a gentler fade.*

Hue Jitter. *Sets the rate at which
the stroke color switches between the
foreground and background colors.
High values cause more frequent
switches between the two colors.*

Hardness. *Controls the size of the
brush's hard center.*

Scatter. *Determines how brush marks
are distributed in a stroke. A low value
produces a dense stroke; a high value
increases the scattering area.*

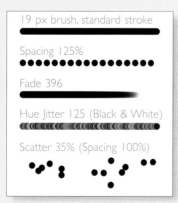

19 px brush, standard stroke

Spacing 125%

Fade 396

Hue Jitter 125 (Black & White)

Scatter 35% (Spacing 100%)

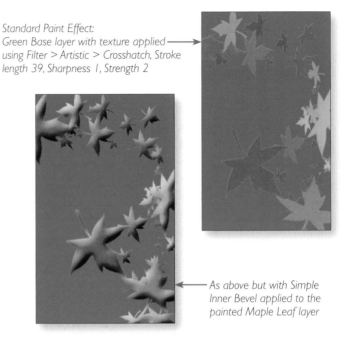

*Standard Paint Effect:
Green Base layer with texture applied
using Filter > Artistic > Crosshatch, Stroke
length 39, Sharpness 1, Strength 2*

*As above but with Simple
Inner Bevel applied to the
painted Maple Leaf layer*

Blend it

Just as you did in Chapters Two and Three you can create amazing effects by painting on multiple layers, rotating layers and changing blending modes and Opacity.

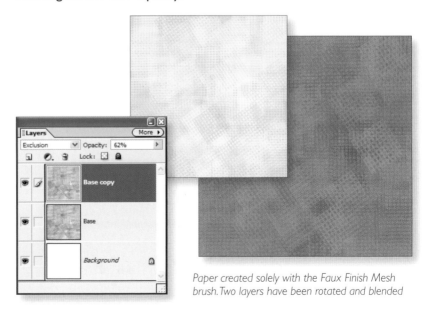

Paper created solely with the Faux Finish Mesh brush. Two layers have been rotated and blended

Torn & Distressed Edges

Torn or distressed edges are common in traditional scrapbooking. In the digital world, simple brush strokes give images the appearance of torn edges.

Smudge it

1 Make a new file. This demonstration uses a six-inch square mini album page

Make a rectangle either by using the Rectangular Marquee tool and filling with color or by using the Shape tool and Simplifying the layer. This example is using black to show the effect more clearly. You can use any color you wish.

2 Make a new layer, name it "Base" and fill it with a pastel color. The example uses R 58, G 249, B 229. You can set these figures in the Color Picker

3 Make a rectangular area on a new layer and fill it with black

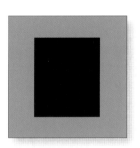 

4 Pick the Smudge tool and a suitable brush. Brushes that work best have lots of texture. Those that work well include the Chalk brushes, Faux and Oil Heavy Dry Edges and Rough Dry Bristle

Some of the brushes are long and thin in shape and may give differing effects along the horizontal and vertical edges. Some brushes can be rotated but it may be easier to rotate the image (Image > Rotate > 90° Left) rather than try and modify the brush.

5 Drag the mouse up and down along the top edge of the black rectangle and the edge will distress. For a softer effect alter the size of the brush and smudge the same area again. You will need to experiment to see what different brushes do and how the brush size changes the result

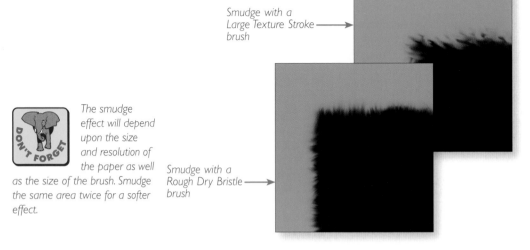

Smudge with a Large Texture Stroke brush

The smudge effect will depend upon the size and resolution of the paper as well as the size of the brush. Smudge the same area twice for a softer effect.

Smudge with a Rough Dry Bristle brush

Paint it

For a stronger edge use the Paint tool and drag the strokes from the solid areas into the transparent areas. Make a note of the technique you like best. You will see the effect in action in later projects.

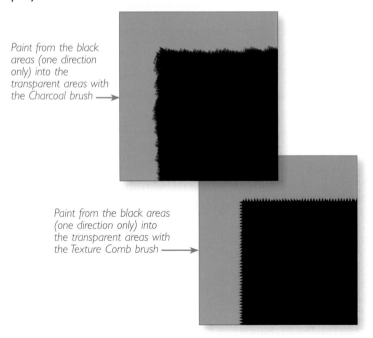

Paint from the black areas (one direction only) into the transparent areas with the Charcoal brush

Paint from the black areas (one direction only) into the transparent areas with the Texture Comb brush

Type & Journaling

A picture is worth a thousand words, so the photographers tell us, but equally words can add significance to your album. The text may simply be a heading or a quote, but it could be much more emotive. Particularly with Heritage pages personal memories and recollections are very important.

Covers

Chapter Six

FlowersEnd.jpg

Cardrona.jpg

Type – Horizontal & Vertical

Cardrona.jpg © John Slater

Where would the scrapbooker be without type? Words are used in many ways. At their simplest they can add a title or a couple of lines to describe the page. Slightly more informative is a caption to tell who, when, where, why or what is in the picture. More words tell a story and this is particularly important in heritage layouts. On a more emotive level are quotes and phrases that express mood and feeling. Last but not least are text elements. These can either create sophisticated border decorations or inject some light-hearted fun into your pages with speech bubbles.

This chapter starts with a mini project and looks at basic type. Later you will discover more creative uses of text and one or two crazy effects. To start, imagine you have been on a fun day out with the kids and now you want a simple memory based around a single photograph. The image you will use has already been manipulated in Photoshop.

Up, Down or Across?

All new images start with only one layer and this is called Background.

1 Open the file Cardrona.jpg and pick the Type tool. This is the one with the big letter T. Press and hold down the mouse to reveal the four choices of type tool. Choose the top one – the Horizontal Type Tool. Set the font, size and color in the Options bar. This example uses a font appropriately called Kids

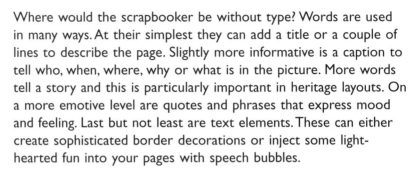

The Horizontal Type tool will type from left to right. The Vertical Type tool will type from top to bottom.

2 Move the mouse over the image (anywhere is OK) and notice that the cursor changes shape to what is called an I-beam. Click to create an insertion point and start typing – just as you would in a word processing program

3 In the Layers palette you will see that a new layer is automatically created each time you start to type, and shows the text you have typed. Type this text:

Chrissie & Greg's (press the Return key)
fun day at Cardrona

Type Tool Options

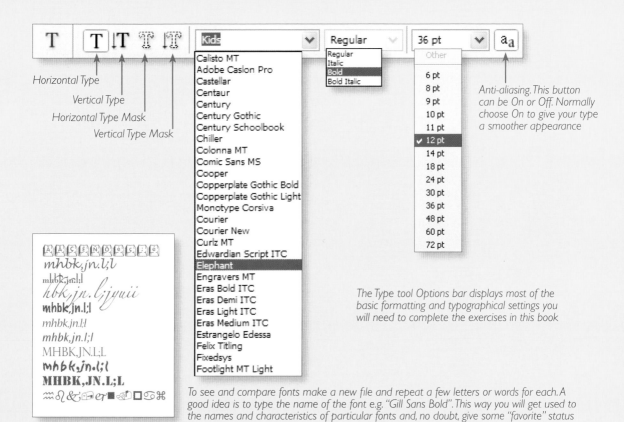

Horizontal Type

Vertical Type

Horizontal Type Mask

Vertical Type Mask

Anti-aliasing. This button can be On or Off. Normally choose On to give your type a smoother appearance

The Type tool Options bar displays most of the basic formatting and typographical settings you will need to complete the exercises in this book

To see and compare fonts make a new file and repeat a few letters or words for each. A good idea is to type the name of the font e.g. "Gill Sans Bold". This way you will get used to the names and characteristics of particular fonts and, no doubt, give some "favorite" status

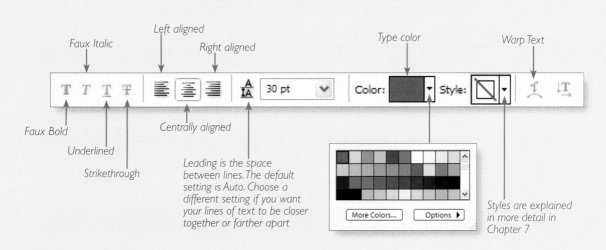

Faux Italic

Left aligned

Right aligned

Type color

Warp Text

Faux Bold

Underlined

Strikethrough

Centrally aligned

Leading is the space between lines. The default setting is Auto. Choose a different setting if you want your lines of text to be closer together or farther apart

Styles are explained in more detail in Chapter 7

4 Press the Enter key and see the changes in the Layers palette. You could also click the Commit button in the Options bar

Type appears on its own layer, shown by the large letter T

If you click on an image with the Type tool and do nothing, a new layer is still created. By default this is called Layer 1. The easiest remedy is to delete this layer.

5 In the Layers palette there are now two layers. At this stage, they are independent of each other. The type has appeared on the image – probably in the wrong place, and perhaps the wrong color. Don't worry! Just highlight the text and make any corrections. To move the text pick the Move Tool in the Toolbox and simply drag the text to where you want it. You can even rotate or distort the text with the Transform tools

6 Pick the Vertical Type tool and a different font. The one used here is Lucida Console. Type "May 2005" and reposition it down the right edge of the page as shown below

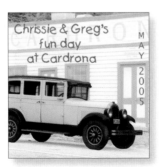
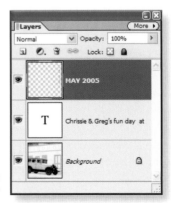

When type layers are Simplified or changed into pixels the big letter T disappears. You need to do this if you want to apply filters to the text

Warp Text

So far it's pretty simple. Now add some funky text to the car door.

Text on a curve and more

1 Type the words "C & G (Return) Taxi Service"

2 Click the Warp Text button, in the Options bar, to reveal its dialog box. This allows you to distort text in many interesting ways

In Photoshop you can type on a curve or along a path of any shape. This is not possible in Photoshop Elements.

3 From the Style drop-down list choose Arc Lower. Move the text into position over the door. You may have to change the size of the text

4 In the Layers palette change the blending mode and the Opacity as shown. Save the file and close it

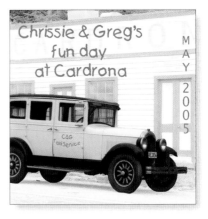

Putting Pictures into Type

Flowers.jpg © John Slater

Scrapbooking is full of interesting text effects. Here is one that looks real cool but is simplicity itself. The effect suits bold type.

Flower Power

1   Open the file Flowers.jpg. Unusually, you are going to create the effect before adding the image to your layout

2   Pick the Horizontal Type Mask tool and type "Mary's Flowers". Initially the image will be covered with a red mask, but when you "commit" the type, this changes to a selection

3   You now have several choices. Choice one is to pick the Move tool and drag the selection to a new document as shown below left

Start tying with the cursor on the right-hand side of the image.

4   Choice two is to delete the selection. The color that appears will be your background color, as shown above right

5   The more sophisticated option is to copy the selection onto a new layer and add further effects or elements. From the menu choose Layer > New > Layer via Copy. The selection appears on its own layer

6 Move this around the image. Already it's interesting, but, perhaps, the new text needs a little more definition. Apply a stroke with Edit > Stroke outline Selection. Choose 5 pixels and a color of your choice

7 To step further away from reality apply a filter to the flower layer with Filter > Artistic > Cutout. Use the settings shown below

For even more definition place a vellum layer between the text and the background as explained on page 112

Putting Pictures into Type: 2

This short exercise is based around Photoshop. If you try to edit the file in Photoshop Elements you will get a warning.

The majority of effects shown in this book can be created with just about any image editing software. Some special effects, however, need more sophisticated programs such as Photoshop to create the fascinating blend effect shown below.

Do your stuff, Jack!

1 Open the file Flowers.jpg

2 Pick the Horizontal Type tool and type "Jack's Garden." The color of the type will have a direct influence on the effect

3 From the menu choose Layer > Layer Styles > Blending Options. The very large and complex-looking Layer Style box appears

Double-click on the Background layer to change it into a standard layer. You can then move it above the text layer.

4 At the bottom of the box find Underlying Layer and move the slider inwards as shown. The effect will depend upon the color of the text and where the text is on the image. Regardless, the effect is remarkable

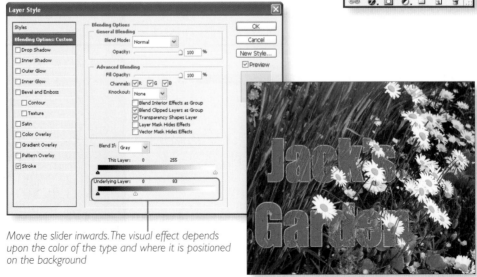

Move the slider inwards. The visual effect depends upon the color of the type and where it is positioned on the background

Talk Bubbles

It's easy and fun to create talk or speech bubbles. Although you can make your own from scratch it is much easier to use or modify those already supplied with the software.

Bubbles in Photoshop Elements

1 Make a new file. Any size will do. The one used here is 5 × 7 inches from the preset list

2 Select the Custom Shape tool. If the Talk Bubbles are not shown in the list, add them

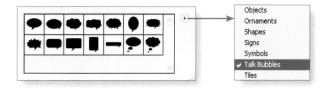

3 Choose a bubble and drag the mouse over your empty file. You can make the bubble as big or as small as you like

4 If the color is not as you want, change it in the Options bar. If the shape is not as you want, change it with Image > Transform Shape > Free Transform Shape

The bubble appears on its own layer – so it is a good idea to have the Layers palette open.

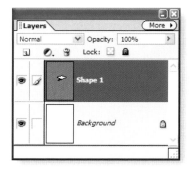

Transformed shape

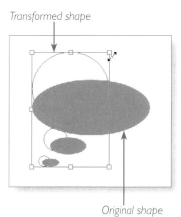

Original shape

5 If you want to add filters or patterns to the bubbles, or for that matter to any custom shape, the shape will have to be converted to pixels first. In Photoshop Elements this is known as Simplifying the layer

In some imaging programs changing shape or text layers into pixels is termed rasterization.

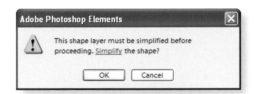

The layer changes appearance when it is Simplified

Other Ideas

Notice the difference in the Layers palette when shapes are Simplified.

Add fun text to the bubble

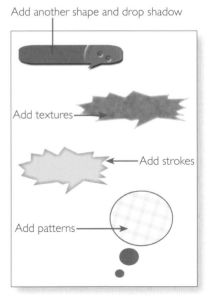

Add another shape and drop shadow

Add textures

Add strokes

Add patterns

Handwriting?

Postcard.jpg
courtesy Vicki Turnbull

The other side of the postcard

It may be argued that adding your own handwriting will enhance the image and that using computer-generated type loses some of the personality. Heritage pages in particular usually benefit from some personal input. For the reluctant, the computer offers scores of typefaces that mimic handwriting. Choose whichever suits the image and your own skills.

What is beyond discussion is the inclusion of letters and postcards that tell fascinating tales and stories. If these are in a poor condition it is unwise to stick them into an album. It's better to use a digital copy that can also be enhanced so that the text is much more legible. The exercise shows a simple two-step process.

From Across the Sea

1 Open the file Postcard.jpg. The signs of decay are obvious. The brown is a sure indication of acid in the paper and eventually this will cause the complete destruction of the card. From the menu select Image > Enhance > Remove Color Cast. A box appears with additional instructions. Follow these

2 Improve the tonal range with Enhance > Adjust Lighting > Levels. Move the sliders to the positions shown below. Save the file as Postcard2.tif. The text now has more contrast and is easier to read

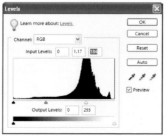

Text Dominating the Page

You cannot add filter effects directly to type. Text appears in most programs as Vector graphics. These need to be converted to pixels for effects to take place. The process of conversion is known as rasterization but in many programs such as Photoshop Elements this happens when you Simplify a layer.

Filling a background page with text is a very common approach by paper manufacturers in traditional scrapbooking. This could be as simple as a single word repeated at random, perhaps at different sizes, different colors, or using different fonts. This is easily done by making a pattern as shown on page 86, and then filling the page with the word pattern. A similar approach is to use several associated words appearing at random over the page. The words could appear floating over a distressed or watermarked background. Text is often overlapped and Opacity changed. Words can also be patterns.

Another common approach is to use quotations or dictionary definitions to fill the page. This effect is shown below. To add to the scene snowflake shapes have been added and these have been given glows and bevels. The captions provide all the detail should you wish to try this effect yourself.

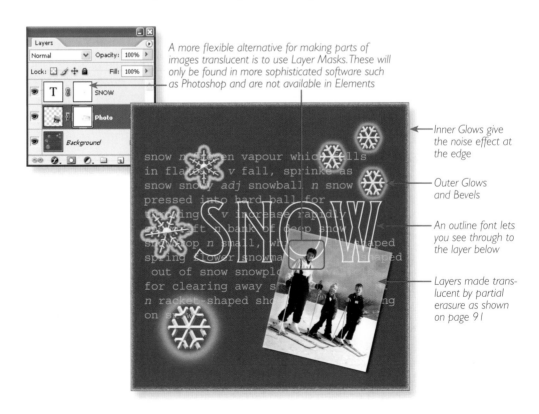

A more flexible alternative for making parts of images translucent is to use Layer Masks. These will only be found in more sophisticated software such as Photoshop and are not available in Elements

Inner Glows give the noise effect at the edge

Outer Glows and Bevels

An outline font lets you see through to the layer below

Layers made translucent by partial erasure as shown on page 91

Another popular approach is to make the text distressed. Traditional scrapbookers do this by gently rubbing the page or individual letters with sandpaper, in effect removing part of the surface. This is not really necessary on the computer because there is a vast array of fonts available that already mimic the distressed look. However, if you want your own unique appearance this is how you do it.

1 Type some words on a page. Automatically the text appears on its own layer, which is important

Elizabeth

Many distressed fonts are available on the internet. The one above is called Khaki

Elizabeth

Plain type, Impact font

2 Pick the Eraser tool and a textured brush. Set the opacity (strength of the eraser) low and gently work over the text. Part will be removed

Elizabeth

Color partially removed using the Eraser at low opacity and a texture brush

3 Change the brush and opacity and work over the text again. How far you go is up to you

Elizabeth

Change the brush and the opacity for additional distressing. A stroke has also been added

Other Ideas

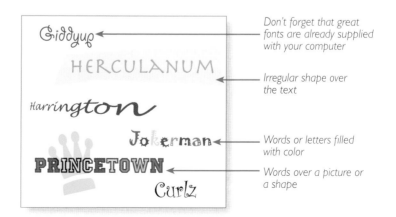

Don't forget that great fonts are already supplied with your computer

Irregular shape over the text

Words or letters filled with color

Words over a picture or a shape

Vellum – Translucent Paper

Blueflowerspattern.jpg

Vellum and parchment are made from animal skin. Vellum in particular tends to have grain or texture and may be irregular in appearance. In scrapbooking vellum often refers to translucent material, with or without texture. In digital scrapbooking, this is achieved by changing the Opacity of a layer. As always there are ways to make your digital vellums look more realistic.

Torn Edge

1 Open the file Blueflowerspattern.jpg. Make a rectangle on a new layer approximately one inch inside the edge of the page and fill it with yellow. Call this new layer Vellum

2 Distress the edge of the rectangle with the Eraser. Try using texture brushes for a less regular edge

3 Enhance the edge. Select the Vellum layer with the Magic Wand and apply a stroke

4 To make the vellum look more realistic reduce the Opacity

Instead of a stroke you may want to try the Burn tool to darken the edges.

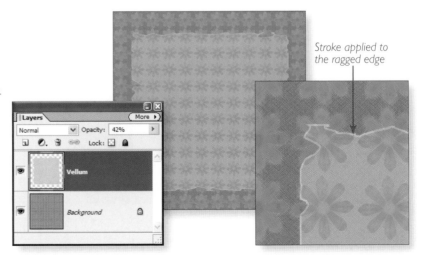

Stroke applied to the ragged edge

5 Text is often applied to vellum. This example uses a short poem by Elizabeth Barrett Browning. Use white paint and, if necessary, reduce the opacity

6 As a further embellishment ornamental Shapes can be added. A neat trick is to delete part of the vellum to reveal the underlying pattern. Do this by first making a Shape. The Shape used in the example is Hedera1

7 Make a selection of the Shape and then hide or delete the Shape layer. Make the Vellum layer active and then delete the selection using the Delete or Backspace key

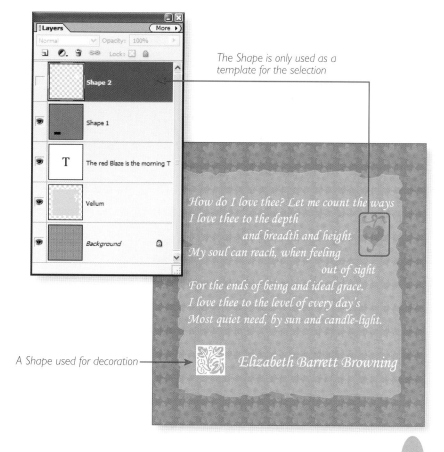

The Shape is only used as a template for the selection

A Shape used for decoration

How do I love thee? Let me count the ways
I love thee to the depth
                and breadth and height
My soul can reach, when feeling
                            out of sight
For the ends of being and ideal grace.
I love thee to the level of every day's
Most quiet need, by sun and candle-light.

Elizabeth Barrett Browning

Type on the Internet

Check out some of the websites listed in Chapter 13.

Although lots of interesting fonts come as standard with your computer they may not quite fit the mood of a particular project. The internet is a veritable "Aladdin's Cave" for the font hunter. There are fonts of all shapes and sizes. A great majority are free. Commercial digital scrapbooking sites offer truly amazing fonts for very little cost.

As just one example, the last project in the book uses an old-fashioned typewriter font. You could use Courier as suggested in the text but why not experiment with the hundreds of specific fonts available. Look at www.desktoppub.about.com and see the virtual mountain of typewriter fonts that are available. Just download and install one, and use it like any other font.

Other typefaces may not strictly be fonts. You can buy Alphabet sets that you will have to place individually on your layout. Such is the case with the set known as greenplaidalpha from www.matterofscrap.com, shown below.

Individual letters assembled on a blank file, transformed to make them a little thinner, some rotated and then all layers merged to keep the word on a single layer

Remember all digital files can be easily and quickly changed to suit your layout. Here a greenplaidalpha letter has been changed to blue with Hue/Saturation, and the stamp effect has been applied with the Cookie Cutter

Fantastic words and decoration at the click of a button. This download is from www.cottagearts.net

Elements & Embellishments

Elements are the bits and pieces that add to the story and are often personal – train tickets, menus, brochures etc. In traditional terms these are referred to as embellishments. In the digital world they are "elements." This chapter shows you how to make some easy elements and how to modify others downloaded from the internet. Use the internet as a source of good, well designed elements, especially if you are new to digital design. This is where you start to learn some of the creative secrets for scrapbooking and concentrate on simple effects that will give your layouts the "wow" factor.

Covers

Chapter Seven

TilesEND.psd

Gymnast.jpg

What are Elements?

You can buy digital elements on the internet or make them yourself, but what are they? Elements are the bits and pieces that add character or personal touches to your layout. The page shown is Prestopage-top-layer from www.matterofscrap.com and will give you an idea of what you can do or what you can buy. The elements shown come as a complete kit but it is possible to purchase individual components.

Flowers, scanned or photographed and cut out of the background

Brads

Text

Tags

Paint Swatches

Ribbons

Finished Layout

Text Rings

Layer Styles

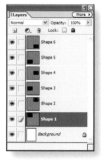

Tiles.psd

Layer Styles are great. They are your gateway to smart effects, and the good news is that all you have to do is press buttons – the software does the rest. You will start with a very simple exercise to see what amazing effects are waiting for your projects. Later, you will see how styles are applied in a realistic way and how they can be modified.

One Button Does it All

1 Open the file Tiles.psd. This file contains six similar shape elements

2 Select Layer 1, the top left tile

3 Navigate to Wow Chrome in the Styles & Effects palette. Click on any of the options to see instant change in the image

4 For each layer in turn simply set the styles shown below

Photoshop offers more sophistication than Photoshop Elements in that all aspects of Styles can be controlled.

Wow Chrome

Wow Neon
Wow–Dk Blue
On

Patterns > Angled
Spectrum

Complex >
Cactus

Patterns > Satin
Overlay plus
Patterns > Waves

Complex >
Color Target

Creative use of Layer Styles

Time to put Layer Styles to the test. You will make a variety of beveled-edge frames using styles and then add type with additional styles and effects.

Chrome Heaven?

If you make the rectangle with the Shapes tool, Simplify it straight away.

1 Make a new file 2 inches by 3 inches and fill it with any color

2 In the Layer Styles palette click on Wow Chrome Beveled Edge. You will get something similar to the image shown top right

3 Color the center of the frame with a simple colored shape or a filled selection

4 Add texture using Filters and a Soft Stripe gradient with the Gradient tool

5 Add a single bold letter and apply a Layer Effect

Center selected and colored purple. Gentle Noise and Crosshatch applied, followed by Soft Stripes with the Gradient tool. Text has an Inner Bevel and an Inner Glow applied plus a Noise filter

Center selected and colored black. Gentle Noise applied. Text has Pillow Emboss and Color Halftone filters applied

Fill a new layer with color. Draw a rectangle inside this and delete it to end up with a border or frame. Add Outer Glow Noisy and Complex Cactus. Text has an Inner Bevel and an Inner Glow applied plus a Noise filter

Change Internet Elements

Many downloads from the internet are free, so you really do not have any excuse not to try a few and pep up your layouts. The slide mount used here was downloaded from escrappers.com. It's free!

www.escrappers.com

Go Surfing

1 Go to www.escrappers.com and download the file Slide template

2 Open the Layers palette and notice there are two layers. Fill the top mount with blue and the bottom mount with a darker version of the same color

3 Select the top layer with the Magic Wand and add some fun color with Filter > Color Halftone

4 Insert pictures into the blank central space as shown on page 70. Drag images onto the slide mount and resize them. Change the stack order as shown on page 47. Flatten layers and Save

Change a Scanned Element

Greenwich.jpg

For the more adventurous you can modify scanned images. Here you are shown how to make "pop art" film strips from a single piece of film.

Pronounced Grenitch!

1. Open the file Greenwich.jpg. This is a scanned transparency that is the base for this short exercise

2. Firstly, you need to straighten and crop the image. It is most unlikely that you will scan all your photos perfectly straight. Pick the Crop Tool and drag over the image. Move the mouse outside the crop box and a double-headed arrow appears. Move the mouse and the box will rotate. Adjust it to fit. Accept the crop by pressing the Enter key

A film template can be downloaded for free from www. escrappers.com, but it is much more fun to make your own!

Mouse cursor

The Shield color shows the area lost with the crop. You can change it to any color you like

Alternatively you can accept the crop by pressing the Commit button in the Options bar.

3. Make a new file 4 x 6 inches (100 mm x 150 mm) and 300 ppi resolution. Drag the straightened image onto the blank file

4. Select the picture area with the Rectangular Marquee and fill it with white. Paint out any wording on the rebate with black. You should have something looking like the image at the top left of the next page

5 You may be happy with a single frame but multiple frames are much more fun. Open the Layers palette and duplicate the film-strip layer (Layer > Duplicate Layer)

You can click on the More button in the Layers palette to Duplicate layers, Flatten Images and Merge layers instead of using the menu.

6 Position the two film-strip frames side by side and from the Layers palette menu select Merge Down. Repeat as many times as you like

7 Select the frame edges and add wacky colors and texture using Filters

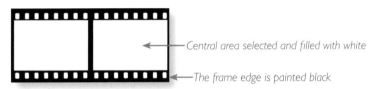

Central area selected and filled with white

The frame edge is painted black

Select the sprocket holes and delete them for a realistic 3D effect. Enhance the frame further with drop shadows and other layer effects.

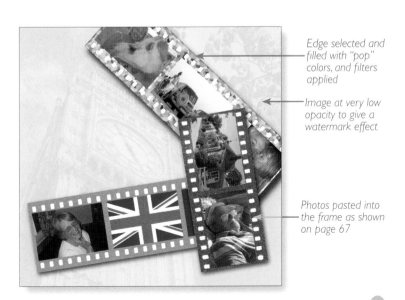

Edge selected and filled with "pop" colors, and filters applied

Image at very low opacity to give a watermark effect

Photos pasted into the frame as shown on page 67

Stencils & Edging

Floral Ornament 2

Just as in real life, stencilling on the computer is applied freehand with a brush to give an individual craft feel. You can scan stencils that you already own but here you will use the Ornament Custom Shapes.

Stipple, Stipple, Click, Click (Method 1)

1 For this short exercise start with a small file. The example uses a six-inch square mini album page

2 Pick the Custom Shapes tool and find the Floral Ornament 2. Draw a single shape filling most of the page. Name this layer Template. Color it red and save it as Template.psd

3 Change the foreground color to lavender. Pick the Brush tool and the Pastel on Charcoal brush. Set a size of 100 pixels and an Opacity of 30% in the Options bar

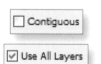

4 Make a new layer and call it Stencil. Pick the Magic Wand and set the Options bar as shown left

5 With the Stencil layer active, click on the red shape and a selection of the whole shape is made. Turn off the visibility of the Template layer by clicking on the eye. Only the selection should be visible

6 Start clicking with the mouse on the inner part of the selection. This action and the choice of brush gives the stippling effect so common in real-life stencilling. Increase the Opacity and paint the outside of the shape. You should end up with something like this

Reset Tool
Reset All Tools

Blend layers for great stencils

Stipple, Stipple, Click, Click (Method 2)

Make a selection in the same way as in Method 1, but this time use standard brushes. The key is to put different shades or different colors on separate layers. The color is applied in strokes not stipples.

1 Use the existing Template file. Make a new layer and call it Base

2 Make the selection and fill it with a lavender color. Lower the Opacity to 21% or lower

3 Make a new layer, call it Middle-Top and apply more paint to the middle–top part of the stencil. The two layers should be distinctly different in color

4 Make another new layer and call it Edges. Change the foreground color to blue and apply more paint to the edges of the stencil. The image and Layers palette should look something like this

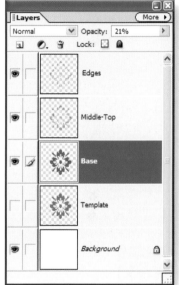

Border Heaven

It looks great and all you have to do is make one stencil and then duplicate it several times in a similar fashion to the Filmstrip exercise on page 121. Simply fun!

Tags

Tags are one of the most common elements found in scrapbooking. It is easy to scan and modify an existing tag, the sort of thing attached to your luggage at the airport. Much more fun, however, is to make one yourself using shapes.

Let's Play Tag

1 Open a new file. For this exercise a 4 x 6 inch page will be fine. Rotate the page to give a landscape shape

2 Pick the Rounded Rectangle Tool and draw a shape on the right-hand side of the page

3 Change to the Polygon Tool, set 6 sides in the Options bar, and draw a shape on the left side of the page. Your image should look something like this:

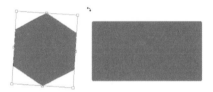

Rather than make your own, download tags from the internet. This tag is available for free download from www.cottagearts.net. The original color has been changed with the Hue/Saturation command. Create your own version of this tag by making the basic shape in the exercise and then pasting in another image as described on page 67.

4 Overlap the shapes and if necessary transform them to fit

5 Turn off the visibility of the Background layer in the Layers palette and Merge Visible. The two shapes become one and are Simplified at the same time. This is your basic template. Once you have this shape you can create all sorts of amazing effects

Shape up

1 Select the tag with the Magic Wand and use Select > Modify > Contract. The selection moves inwards

Change color with Hue/Saturation and add borders

Set the Stroke width and color in the stroke dialog box.

2 Select > Stroke outline Selection. A thin line is applied

3 With the Elliptical Selection tool make a small circle for the hole. Press the delete key. Your tag is now taking shape!

4 It's looking good but needs some depth. Just pick Simple Bevel from the Styles and Effects palette for a dramatic change

Add bevels with Styles and Effects

5 Now apply images, shapes and filters on new layers and blend as you have done elsewhere in the book. Here are some ideas:

Flower pattern created on page 88 added on a new layer. Cutout filter applied and blend mode changed to Screen. Opacity lowered to 43. Single flower added on new layer with Inner Glow

Have fun experimenting. Try combining all sorts of interesting shapes to create amazing tags. Here the Twirl and Rounded Rectangle shapes join forces.

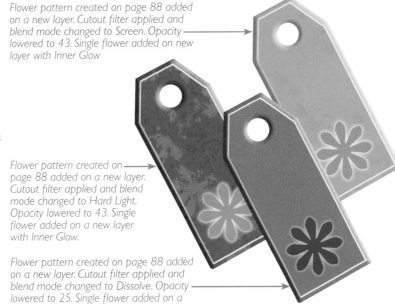

Flower pattern created on page 88 added on a new layer. Cutout filter applied and blend mode changed to Hard Light. Opacity lowered to 43. Single flower added on a new layer with Inner Glow.

Flower pattern created on page 88 added on a new layer. Cutout filter applied and blend mode changed to Dissolve. Opacity lowered to 25. Single flower added on a new layer with Inner Glow.

Ribbons

Making tags is a pretty simple operation compared to making ribbons. Initially you may want to think about scanning ribbons that you already have, or perhaps buy a few ready-prepared digital files. Those shown below are from www.matterofscrap.com.

Let's get in a tangle

1. Open a new file. A long thin 2 x 5 inch page will be fine. The background should be set to transparent. Rotate the page to give a landscape shape. Change the name of the layer to Base

2. Set two similar colors for the foreground and the background. The example uses R244, G47, B47 and R245, G143, B143. These colors are set in the Color Picker

3. Make a long thin rectangular selection, about half the height of the file, and fill it with color

Transparent

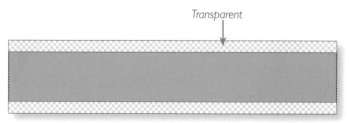

4 Generate a striped effect with Filter > Sketch > Halftone Pattern. Set the options as shown below:

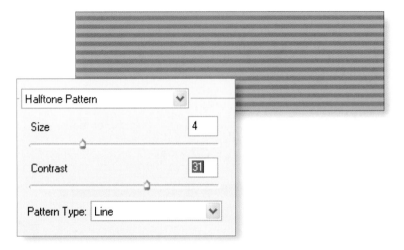

5 Add gentle texture with Filter > Noise followed by Filter > Brush Strokes > Crosshatch as shown below:

Rather than burn freehand use the computer to help you keep a consistent straight line. Set the Burn tool options. Click on the top left corner of the ribbon and click. Move to the top right corner, hold down the shift key, and click again. The top edge is darkened or burnt. Repeat if necessary. This technique works with all the painting tools.

6 Pick the Burn tool at maximum strength and a 21-pixel hard, round brush, and "paint" along both edges

7 Make a new layer. Set the foreground to white. Pick the Gradient tool and choose Special Effects Soft Stripes. Drag a gradient along the length of the ribbon. Lower the Opacity to 48% and change the blending mode to Color Burn. This gives a gentle rippled effect. Merge the two layers with Layers > Merge Visible

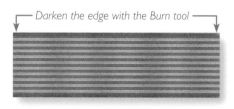

Darken the edge with the Burn tool

8 Add gentle curves to the ribbon with Filter > Distort > Wave. Use the settings shown below. Try other variations. Nothing to it, really!

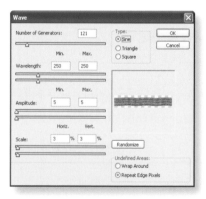

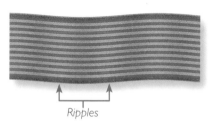

Ripples

Add shapes to the ribbon and a Noisy Glow

Change the Wave Type to triangle for this interesting edge effect. Make sure the Canvas size is wide enough to accept the new ribbon. Color was changed using Hue/Saturation. Make the ribbon thinner by using the Transform commands

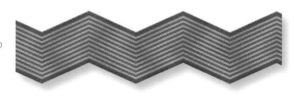

Intertwining Hearts

Heart Frame Custom Shape

As you get more adventurous with your layouts you will want elements to look more realistic. Shadows and bevels are a great help in establishing the illusion, but other tricks are easy as shown next. You will create the illusion of two hearts intertwining. Follow all the steps using the illustrations on the next two pages.

Hearts are forever

In the example the foreground color is white.

1 Open a small file: a 4 × 5-inch file will be adequate

2 Make a new layer and fill it with a lavender color: R191, G176, B199

3 Pick the Custom Shapes tool and find the "Heart Frame" shape. Drag to create a heart about half the size of the page

4 Choose Simple Inner Bevel in the Styles and Effects palette. In the same palette change the Visibility to Ghosted

You can move the Layers palette to any location you like by dragging the palette tab.

5 Change the color of the heart to CMYK Magenta (in Swatches)

6 Click on the little ⓕ in the Layers palette to reveal the Style setting box and change the Bevel Size to 68 and Lighting Angle to 115. These changes will give the heart more depth

7 Duplicate the Heart layer and move the copy to the right, but keep the shapes overlapped

8 Apply Filter > Pixelate > Pointillize to the top heart. You will be asked to Simplify the layer first. The example uses a Cell Size of 42. Reapply the Bevel that was lost when the filter was applied

9 Pick the Eraser. Simply erase one of the overlapping areas. You need a steady hand to get a good result

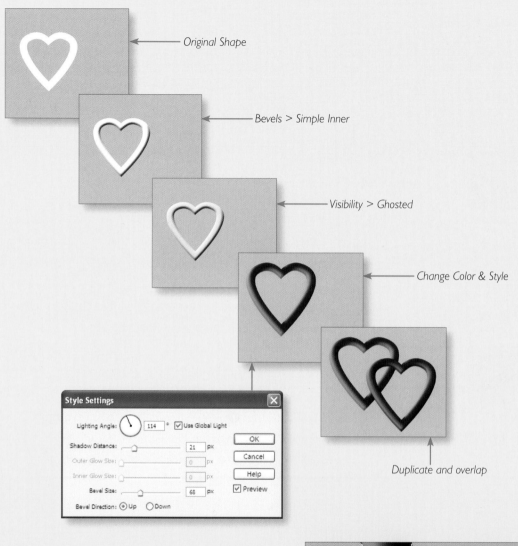

Original Shape

Bevels > Simple Inner

Visibility > Ghosted

Change Color & Style

Duplicate and overlap

Style Settings

Lighting Angle: [114] ° ☑ Use Global Light

Shadow Distance: —○———— [21] px

Outer Glow Size: ○————— [0] px

Inner Glow Size: ○————— [0] px

Bevel Size: ———○——— [68] px

Bevel Direction: ⊙ Up   ○ Down

[OK]
[Cancel]
[Help]
☑ Preview

Erase part of the top heart to give
the impression that the shapes are
interlocking. To maintain a smooth
edge make a selection of the top
heart before erasing

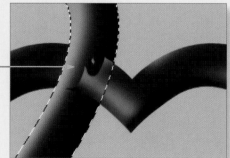

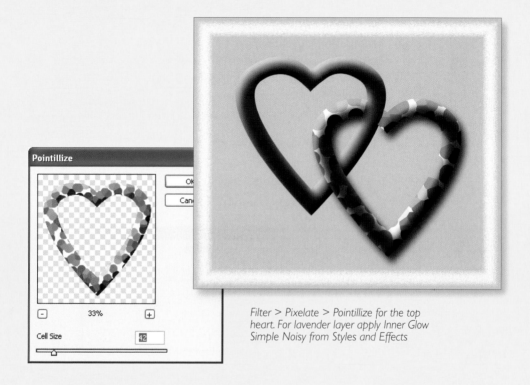

Filter > Pixelate > Pointillize for the top
heart. For lavender layer apply Inner Glow
Simple Noisy from Styles and Effects

Photoshop offers much more
specific control than Photoshop
Elements. Here individual
shadows have been changed

Gymnastic Hoops – Mini Project

Gymnast.jpg
© Carolyn Lamb-Miller

Imagine it's school sports day and you have a budding gymnast competing, perhaps even a future Olympic Champion. In this mini project you will embellish an existing photo with hoops or rings, similar to those found in Rhythmic Gymnastics. You will also discover how to cut an image out of its background. Your skills with the Selection and Eraser tools will be enhanced.

Cut-Away the Background

1 Make a new file the size of a mini album and fill with color. This example uses a blue color, R44, G177, B240

2 Open the file Gymnast.jpg and drag onto the colored file. You may wish to make the Gymnast a little smaller

3 Eliminate the background using the Background Eraser tool. Pick the tool and set the Options as shown below:

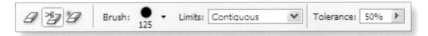

4 Carefully work around the gymnast taking care not to erase any of the body. If you do then Edit > Undo immediately

5 When the circuit is complete change to the Magic Eraser and click in the unwanted white background to make it disappear!

6 Save the file as Gymnast2.psd to retain the transparency. You will need it to complete the next section

Photoshop users may prefer to use the sophisticated Extract tool to create cutouts.

Drag the Background eraser all the way around the Gymnast taking care to keep the center of the brush JUST outside the subject. Change to the Magic Eraser to clean up

Through the Hoops

Now you will add graphic elements to make the image more colorful, but take care. If you use the same method as shown on page 130 you will be in trouble when you apply shadows and bevels. Clever use of layers comes to the rescue.

1 Pick the Custom Shapes tool and find the "Circle Frame". Choose a suitable color and drag a large circle – the size of a hula-hoop

2 Distort the circle to give it perspective using Image > Transform Shape > Distort. Position the "hoop" under the gymnast's feet

You may have to alter the Layer order to get the hoop beneath the feet, or in front of the arms.

3 Make a smaller hoop, distort and position over the gymnast's left arm. It should appear in front of the arm

Make sure you are on the correct layer.

4 Instead of erasing part of the hoop the trick is to copy part of the arm. Since the gymnast has a transparent background this is easy. Make a selection with the Rectangular Marque and then use Layer > New > Layer via Copy. Move the small selection above the hoop shape in the Layer stack. Magic! Repeat for the right arm

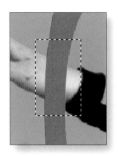

Enhance

To complete this exercise add some text and enhance with Layer Styles and Effects.

1 Make the background more interesting. The example uses blue to gray textured gradient

2 Add a caption. The font used here is called Herculanum

3 Add bevels, shadows etc. to all layers for realism

4 Flatten the image and save it. Do you deserve a gold medal?

Text with bevels and drop shadows

New gradient background with texture

Subject cut out of original background and drop shadow added

Shapes with drop shadows and bevels

Improve and Enhance your Photos

Once you get into scrapbooking, in any form, you will almost certainly think of projects to create from scratch rather than making albums from existing images. Every time you go on holiday or to an event at the local school, new ideas present themselves. Always have your camera ready to capture interesting pictures and remember to collect mementos to scan for your elements.

Keep focused and don't try to photograph everything. By concentrating on one theme at a time you will have more choice and, importantly, better images. It may be as simple as shooting with the camera vertically as well as horizontally.

Covers

Auckland.jpg   *ThreeMoreFairies.jpg*   *Faint.jpg*   *TeamSA.jpg*   *Damaged.jpg*

Composition – Look & Learn

The hardest part of photography is arranging your subjects so that they feel comfortable and look interesting. You can influence people by asking them to move or to alter their stance. Sometimes you, as the photographer, will have to move and change viewpoint. If you plan to cut a subject out of its background make the computer work easy by choosing simple, uncluttered surroundings.

Improve your Composition

Turn your camera on its side to get a shape that best suits the picture →

← *Encourage the subjects to relate to each other*

Look right to the edges of your viewfinder. Check for unwanted objects. Eliminate them by zooming in, or changing the camera's viewpoint.

Don't leave too much empty space around the photo and encourage subjects to be expressive and animated

Relax your subject by getting them to do something rather than standing still. Here clever use has been made of a simple fence. Use props to reinforce your photos

Chop, Chop – the Crop Tool

ThreemoreFairies.jpg
© Lisa Thornley

If you want to crop many images to exact measurements enter the dimensions in the Options bar. You also have a choice of preset sizes.

```
Crop Tool 2.5 in x 2 in
Crop Tool 5 in x 3 in
Crop Tool 5 in x 5 in
Crop Tool 6 in x 4 in
Crop Tool 7 in x 5 in
Crop Tool 8 in x 10 in
```

A common fault with many photographers is that they don't fill the frame. When making a traditional album, do you dramatically chop images and throw away lots of excess background? If you find you have to do this with lots of your pictures, then it certainly means that you should get closer at the taking stage. In this exercise you will learn how to crop your images to make them look better.

Scissor Happy

1 Open the file ThreeMoreFairies.jpg. As you can see this has lots of distractions in the background

2 Pick the Crop tool and drag a box over the image as shown. Adjust the crop by dragging the handles. Press Enter/Return to see a much improved picture. As simple as that!

If many of your pictures are improved by cropping, change your taking technique. Compose the picture as normal; then take a couple of paces forward and shoot. Surprise yourself!

Accept the crop by pressing the Enter key or the Commit button in the Options bar

Reject the crop by pressing the Esc key or the Cancel button in the Options bar

The dark "Shield" area shows which parts of the photo will be cropped

Drag the handles to adjust the crop

Get Rid of Busy Backgrounds

ThreemoreFairies.jpg
© Lisa Thornley

Inevitably you will want to make a selection of something that has no strongly defined edges. In such cases, a click with the Magic Wand will be ineffective. The Selection Brush then becomes your ally and like all tools in image editing programs it can be used in a variety of ways. Selections can be made by either "painting" the area you want to change, or "painting" the area you don't want to change. In either case, an existing selection made with the Lasso tool is a good starting point.

Selection Brush

The ThreeMoreFairies file you have just cropped should still be open. As you can see, this still has lots of distractions in the background. Here you will blur the background and make the onlookers less noticeable.

 Sometimes it is easier to select what you do not want and then inverse the selection to get what you do want. This is the case with this exercise. Select the fairies and then select the inverse to blur the background.

1 Pick the Lasso tool and make a rough selection by dragging around the fairies. In the photo (right) some areas are correctly selected, some need adding to the selection and others need removing from the selection

2 Add to the selection by painting with the Selection Brush in Selection mode. Here the fingers are added by painting with a fine brush

3 Subtract from the selection by painting in Mask Mode. Here, painting the red mask between the fingers subtracts from the selection

4 Once the selection is complete soften the edge of the selection. Make sure you are in Selection Mode and use Select > Feather. A setting around 8 should be fine

5 You now have the Fairies selected, but it is the background you need to change. Remedy this with Select > Inverse

Keep the settings low for a more subtle blend.

6 To soften the background use Filter > Blur > Gaussian Blur. Try a setting of about 6. If you want a softer result simply apply the filter again. Then use Select > Deselect

7 If there is a distinct join between the sharp subject and the soft background use the Blur tool to give a gradual blend. Save the file and close

If your camera has suitable controls you can get soft backgrounds at the taking stage by using large apertures, e.g. f4.

If there is a distinct join use the Blur tool at a low setting to create a gradual blend

End result: the distracting background is eliminated and the fairies have a soft "glow"

Viewpoint – Look & Learn

Improve your photographs quickly and dramatically by changing your viewpoint. This is especially good with animals and children. The big rule is to get down to their level. If you can do this and "fill the frame" so much the better. The pictures below of "Rory" illustrate this point precisely.

Bend your Knees!

Original viewpoint standing upright

Down on your knees you will capture a much more powerful picture

The original tag is available for free download from www. cottagearts.net.

Get close for emphasis. You can almost hear Rory's brain ticking!

Use Flash Outside – Look & Learn

Believe it or not it is often advantageous to use your camera's built-in flash when the sun is shining brightly. Strong sun produces strong shadows and the flash minimizes these. The effect is known as fill-in flash. It is also possible to reduce the shadows using the software, as shown in Chapter Twelve, but the results are not quite as effective as using flash in the first place.

Get Flashy

Standard Exposure: shadows tend to be dark and detail is lost

When was the last time you looked at your camera's manual? Check if it is possible to adjust the amount of fill-in flash for even better results.

Standard exposure plus flash: shadows now show more detail

Basic Corrections

The digital process, either in a camera or by scanning, produces imperfections. All digital images can be improved by minor corrections.

Learn this Routine

Auckland.jpg © John Slater

1 Every time you open a digital image you should check the tonal balance. Open Auckland.jpg and select Enhance > Adjust Lighting > Levels

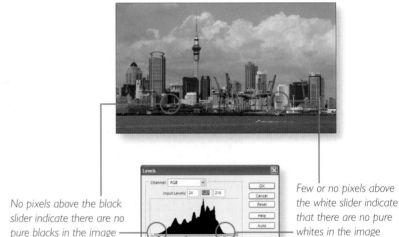

Brightness & Contrast is a simpler alternative to Levels but offers less precise control.

If you make changes to the Levels sliders that you do not like, press the Reset button rather than moving the sliders back or pressing Cancel.

No pixels above the black slider indicate there are no pure blacks in the image

Few or no pixels above the white slider indicate that there are no pure whites in the image

2 A good rule of thumb is to move the sliders inwards until they reach the start of the graph, as shown. Immediately you will see an increase in contrast. This may cause some loss of detail in the mid tones so counter this by moving the middle slider – in this case a little to the left. The image should be vastly improved

The closer the white and black sliders move to each other the more contrast the image will have.

3 With any image personal choice is important. We do not all "see" in the same way. You should find, however, that this image has a pale blue cast. Reduce this by altering the color balance. Look at Enhance > Adjust Color > Color Variations

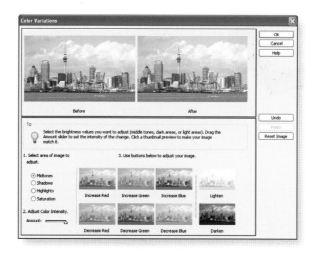

If this is all too baffling try selecting Enhance > Auto Smart Fix from the menu.

Use a soft-edged brush and keep the settings low; build up effects rather than trying to achieve finished results in one go.

4 Play around with this box to discover how the changes affect your image. Regardless of your own personal choice (in this instance) add more yellow (decrease blue) and click OK

5 The image should be looking pretty good, but some emphasis to the clouds will have a dramatic effect. Pick the Burn Tool and gently massage the clouds until they look better

Use a soft brush   *Keep this setting low*

Avoid over sharpening as this will introduce ugly "noise" into the image.

6 Complete the image with sharpening. You will find that most images will benefit from sharpening. From the menu choose Filter > Sharpen > Unsharp Mask

7 Use the settings shown as the basis for your own experiments. Save the file as AucklandEND and close

Scanning

If you don't have a scanner you are missing out. With a scanner you can make high quality copies of images for sharing or restoration. Additionally you can scan objects: stamps, restaurant receipts, tickets, menus etc, and build up a library of embellishments. Better still, you don't have to glue the original into an album. You can also collect images from friends and family to add to your collection. Scan old letters, kids' paintings, newspaper clippings and extracts from diaries and journals. Scanning is easy and fun.

Choosing a Scanner

There are basically three types of scanner:

Anything you scan belonging to or created by others should be credited. Legally you may have to seek permission to copy images out of books, magazines and newspapers to avoid infringing copyright.

1. The cheapest and simplest option is a flatbed scanner that will only scan opaque objects, but will be perfectly good enough for scanning old photos, tickets, maps, journals, solid objects etc.

2. Film scanners are somewhat more specialized. These give very high quality and should be considered if you have to scan a large collection of old slides (transparencies) or negatives.

3. Perhaps the most useful would be a combination scanner that does both jobs. While its film scanning is unlikely to be as good as that of a dedicated film scanner the results should be more than adequate for scrapbooking purposes.

Scan at 300 pixels per inch for photographic quality.

What to Look for

The quality of a scan is largely determined by resolution and bit depth. Most modern scanners will do a decent job but for scrapbookers several points should be considered.

1. **Descreening** If you scan a lot of paper cuttings containing photos a descreening filter, built into the scanner software, will eliminate much of the spotty, pixelated appearance common in newspaper photos. Set the filter according to the quality of the scanned image: for newspapers with a coarse scan use 85, for magazines 133, and for fine printed materials 175.

2. **Color Restoration & Dust Removal** If you have many images that have lots of spots, marks, or are badly faded you may find built-in restoration features useful and could save you many hours of retouching. The most common software, usually included with better scanners, is known as Digital Ice.

Don't be afraid of scanning three dimensional objects. The phone was scanned and the baby picture added as shown on page 68. Below, a memento from a trip to Japan.

Paper clipping courtesy of The Christchurch Press

Newspaper Cuttings

To see the effects of the descreening filter look at scanned newspaper cuttings. Additionally you will enhance the image using Levels and Sharpening.

1 Open Soccer1.jpg and Soccer2.jpg. Position them side by side with Window > Images >Tile

2 Soccer1 is for visual reference only. This has been scanned without a descreening filter. Soccer2.jpg has been scanned with descreening and the result is much smoother, although a little soft. Correct the tonal values by using Enhance > Adjust Lighting > Levels in a similar way to that shown on page 109

3 Improve sharpness with Filter > Sharpen > Unsharp Mask as shown on page 143

No regrets: striker Gareth Turnbull says he loves his college lifestyle in the United States.

Soccer1.jpg shows a scan with the descreening filter off

No regrets: striker Gareth Turnbull says he loves his college lifestyle in the United States.

Soccer2.jpg shows a scan with the descreening filter on

No regrets: striker Gareth Turnbull says he loves his college lifestyle in the United States.

Soccer2.jpg corrected by adjusting Levels so that the text from the page underneath is eliminated

Restore Faded Photos

Faint.jpg

In modern scrapbooking there is an unwritten rule that all images have to be mounted on archival materials or processed to archival standards. But what can you do about those images that are already fading away in the drawer? Help is at hand in the form of digital magic and the crafty use of our friendly layers.

Multiply and Get Twice the Image

1 Open the file Faint.jpg. As you can see this has lost a lot of density and is overall yellow in color

2 Open the Layers palette and click on the More button. From the list choose Duplicate Layer and in the palette see that you have a copy of the image above another copy

Some scanners have a color restore function that, at the touch of a button, has the same effect as this exercise.

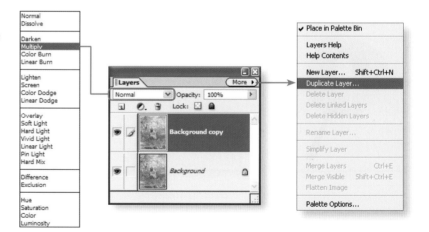

3 From the drop-down list change the blending mode from Normal to Multiply and the image is magically darkened – the two layers are working as one

4 The effect is a little too strong. So use more layer magic. Click on the Adjustment layer button and choose Levels from the list

...cont'd

Adjustment Layers work exactly as their menu counterparts with the same name, but allow the added flexibility that you can make additional changes or remove the effect at the touch of a button. For fine tuning the Opacity setting acts like a fade control.

5 Rather than try and guess the settings let the computer help you. In the Levels dialog find the White Eyedropper in the bottom right corner. Whatever you click on with this tool will become white. The obvious area to choose is the paper edge. Click here and the image becomes similar to what the original would have been

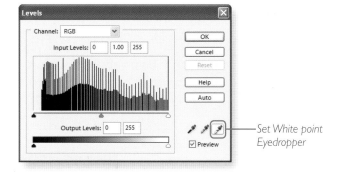

Set White point Eyedropper

If you still shoot photographs on film, buy an 81 filter and use it on cloudy days or when taking pictures in the shade.

6 In reality this makes the image look a little cold, which is exactly what you would expect from a photograph taken in the shade. Add some warmth by using a Photo Filter Adjustment layer. The example uses the 81 filter at its default setting of 25%

7 When you are perfectly happy with the changes, flatten, save and close

Adjustment Layer button

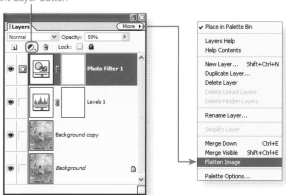

Restore Damaged Photos

Damaged.jpg

Those of you creating memories in the form of heritage scrapbooks will no doubt come across many interesting photos that in many cases, sadly, will be damaged. While the purist may say that these are the ones that should be put into an album, digital offers a distinct advantage. Superb copies can be made easily for sharing among friends and family; the original can be better protected elsewhere. Digital also offers the chance to restore precious originals that, literally, may be falling apart. In the example shown here there is much damage but most of it can be repaired by simply copying from one area to another.

Don't Expect Perfection

1 Open the file Damaged.jpg. The scan is slightly crooked. Square it up using the Crop tool as shown on page 137

Put the mouse outside the crop box to rotate.

Correct a crooked scan by positioning the mouse outside the crop box. A bent double-headed arrow appears. The image will rotate as you move the mouse

Don't try and make old photographs look brand new. Some wear and tear is to be expected and complements the image.

2 Remove the yellow discoloration with Enhance > Remove Color. The image is somewhat flat so adjust it with Enhance > Adjust Lighting > Brightness/Contrast. Try Brightness +15 and Contrast +18

3 Repair the damaged corner by copying a good one – the top left corner looks the best bet. Make an L-shaped selection with the Rectangular Marquee tool

4 Then choose Layer > New > Layer via Copy. A new layer containing this small section appears in the Layers palette. Drag it to the right-hand side of the page and use Image > Rotate > Flip Layer Horizontal

...cont'd

Don't be greedy and try to do it all at once. By repairing small sections you can distort these to get a better fit. Use the Eraser to soften the distinct edges of any repairs.

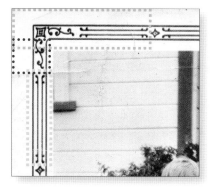

To make a L-shaped selection, first select the area shown in green. Then either hold down the Shift key or check the Add Selection modifier in the Options bar and drag another selection (shown in purple). The two selections become one

Because the copy is on its own layer you can soften any distinct edges with the Eraser set at low Opacity

5 Move the replacement corner into position and if necessary soften any distinct edges with the Eraser. When it all looks good, squash the layers together with Layer > Flatten Image

6 Repeat the process for the section shown above in yellow. Because the edge decoration is not square distort the duplicate with Image > Transform > Distort, for a better fit. Continue this copy routine for other damaged areas around the edge of the photo

Repair the Internal Damage

Many of the small marks and scratches seen all over the photo are easily repaired using the Spot Healing Brush. This copies one part of the image to another in real time.

Zoom into the boy's face and notice there are lots of black and white "spots". Pick the Spot Healing Brush. Change the brush size to about 10 pixels. A brush stroke slightly bigger than the mark seems to work best. Just drag over the mark and it vanishes!

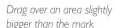

Drag over an area slightly bigger than the mark

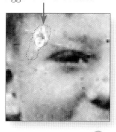

2 For larger defects the Clone Stamp tool will work better. Zoom into the grass beneath the children's feet. Pick the tool and set a brush size of about 30 pixels

Alt+Click means pressing the Alt key and clicking with the mouse. This sets the sample point. It is a good idea to change the sample point every few seconds to avoid the build-up of patterns.

3 Position the mouse just to the left of the large white crease at the bottom of the photo. Alt+Click to set the point you copy **from**. Notice that the cursor changes

4 Position the mouse over the white damage, press and hold down the mouse and drag upwards. The white line is "repaired" as the grass from the left is copied over it

Leave some texture. You still want the photo to look old so there is no need to be fanatical and get rid of every mark.

The cross shows what you are copying — The circle shows where you are copying to

Drag the mouse upwards

5 Repeat this process over other parts of the image. In areas that have straight edges make a selection first. As an example zoom into the dark doorway and with the Polygon Lasso make a selection. This will limit any changes you make to this area

6 Retouching is time consuming but very gratifying when you do it properly. When you do get into a mess, go backwards using the Undo History palette instead of compounding your errors. Enjoy!

Removing Red Eye

TeamSA.jpg © Janine Burgess

The Red Eye Removal tool removes red eye in flash photos of people and yellow-green color in flash photos of animals. The problem is caused by reflections on the back of the retina and occurs more often with photos in dark rooms when the pupils are enlarged. Modern cameras have built-in pre-flash that helps to eliminate this problem by contracting the pupils.

Not so Flash

The Red Eye Removal Tool is available via either the Editor or Quick Fix.

1 Open the file TeamSA.jpg and look carefully. Five of the group have red eyes caused by the flash

2 Zoom into one of the eyes and pick the Red Eye Removal Tool

3 Either click in the red area of the eye or draw a selection. After a short delay the red is eliminated. Some control is offered by the adjustments in the Options bar

Make sure your selection covers all the eye and not just the pupil. The tool is less good at removing the yellow-green cast seen in animals.

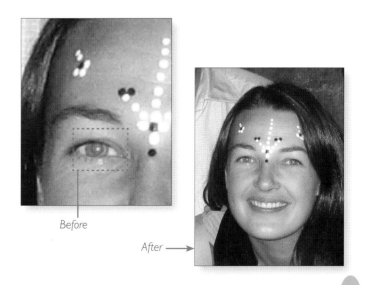

Before

After ⟶

Printers, Paper & Ink

Choosing a Printer   There is a staggering array of printers available, virtually all capable of giving superb quality prints. But which do you choose? It's simple – you need a printer capable of printing pages the size of your album pages. Traditional albums are 12 inches (30.5 cm) square. Be aware that most "standard" printers will only print Letter size (USA), or A4 (Europe, Asia, NZ, Australia).

Laser, inkjet and dye sublimation printers are all capable of results that look good. However, avoid lasers as they only allow a limited choice of media and the archival quality is poor. Dye sublimation printers at the size you need are good but very expensive. The usual choice is the inkjet printer and the big players are Epson, Canon and Hewlett-Packard. Inkjets offer a great range of media.

Archival Quality   Scrapbooking is all about preserving memories and so it is important to use the most fade-resistant materials for your printing. Inkjet materials have improved a lot in the last couple of years and most papers will do a good job.

Epson have led the charge and introduced papers specifically for scrapbookers. Currently these are only available in the USA. These are acid-free, lignin-free, buffered papers; independent tests suggest that prints on them will last up to 200 years in an album, as opposed to 25–75 years with "normal" papers. These papers can also be torn and used in hybrid layouts. The cotton gives a wonderful ragged edge.

Surface Texture   The surface of the paper has a great influence on the "mood" of your pages. Use glossy paper for more contrasty and saturated colors, perfect for parties or sports. Matte papers have slightly subdued colors but a lovely tactile quality. You can also print onto paper that has a canvas texture, very popular for wedding photographs. Traditional scrappers may like to print onto transparent film and use it as an overlay.

Save paper by printing several images on a page. Use Picture Package in Photoshop and Photoshop Elements.

Inks   Inexpensive printers have four color inks. These are OK but will not match the saturation or subtlety of those with more.

There are two basic types of ink: dyes and pigments. Most inexpensive printers use dye inks. These are improving but archival performance may not be up to scrapbooking standards. Some of these prints are only expected to last in pristine condition for 25 years or so. If in doubt, choose pigment inks.

Ready-made Templates

In the next four chapters you will use many of the techniques shown earlier to create finished projects.

The easiest way to get quick results is to use ready-made layouts. You can buy them in a vast array of designs on the internet. Some are even free!

There are basically two types. Templates are the easiest. The page is complete except for the picture. Just add you own and voilá. Offering more flexibility are page kits where each individual element comes on a separate layer. These you can move around and alter to get a quick solution but one matched to your individual taste. To get started, however, look at the templates that are included with your software.

Covers

Kim 1

Kim 2

Kim 3

Kim 4

Chapter Nine

Adobe Photoshop Elements Templates

Adobe Photoshop Elements comes with built-in templates for greeting cards, calendars and, of course, scrapbooks. Let's see how this works.

Party Time

1 From the Photoshop Elements start-up screen click on Create to start the Creation Wizard

2 Choose the layout you want, and the options. In this example pick Photo Album Pages and click OK

All images © Patrick Lauson

3 In the next screen choose the template style you want from the right side of the screen. This example uses "Fun for kids". Add other options such as the number of pages and the number of photos per page. Click Next Step

You can also click the Create button in the Organizer to start the Creation Wizard.

Only saved images can be used.

4 Add the photos. These are displayed in the order they were selected, but you can change the order simply by dragging. In this example the photos are Kim1, 2 and 3. Click Next Step

5 Once the page(s) are generated they can be customized and captions added

6 Name and save the project. Pages are saved in PDF (Portable Document Format) so that just about anybody with a computer can see and print them. PDF files can also be opened in Elements for additional editing

Here are the album pages created in the exercise. The templates are simple and fun, but note that they are not the same size or shape as the traditional album

Flexibility and Choice

The built-in software has a wide range of templates. You can create postcards, calendars or greeting cards in exactly the same way as photo album pages

Templates on the Internet

If you want to go digital but are not yet ready to make all the elements yourself or, perhaps, you find the templates available with the software too limiting, there is a very easy solution – buy ready-made pages. Yes, they do exist, and for just about any theme you could imagine. Pay a visit to some of the websites listed on page 187 and be staggered by the fantastic designs on offer. On the next three pages are a few examples. You will still need some basic understanding about transforming and resizing images if you want the layout to fit your pictures or your pictures to fit the layout.

www.cottagearts.net

Files are usually supplied in JPEG or PNG formats. The latter come as a single layer with transparency, making it easy to put a picture behind. A finished page can be made in seconds

Some pages are provided completely finished. Others leave space for journaling. Pages would normally be flattened for saving and printing

Amazingly complex designs are available from www. mangelsdesigns.com. Below and left are examples from their Victorian pages

www.cottagearts.net

Funny-Shaped Layouts

Look at the frame below from Mangels designs. If you want to add it to a page a little care is needed to preserve the interesting shape. Note that the original has transparency both inside and outside the frame.

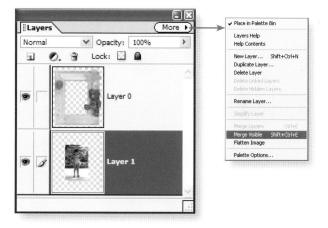

The teddy bear frame is a commercial product and is not available as a free download – sorry!

Drag the photo across and resize it (or vice-versa). Make sure the frame is the top layer and click on the More button. From the list choose Merge Down. This combines the two layers but maintains the transparent edge. If the photo is now dragged onto a new layout the special shape is maintained. On the other hand if the image had been flattened it would have a white edge and the special shape would be lost

Page Kits

A little more adventurous are page kits. These either consist of a layered file where you can adjust individual elements or just a collection of files that you arrange and manipulate to your own taste. In either case the files usually come with suggested layout ideas. The kit shown above is a Heritage pack and is available for free download from www.cottagearts. net. All files come in PNG format. This means that they are already on transparent backgrounds so all you have to do is assemble the elements around your own pictures. You don't have to do very much – even the shadowing is included. You may, however, want to change the color to suit your own images and include one or two elements of your own.

Welcome – Powhiri Project

Now it's time to create a project from scratch. This first project helps you put together some of the techniques shown in the earlier chapters. The page beautifully represents the welcome you may receive if you ever visit the Maori in New Zealand. The welcome ceremony is known as a Powhiri. The gentle touching of noses is called Hongi and symbolizes the sharing of breath in friendship. Welcome to your first complete digital scrapbooking project.

Covers

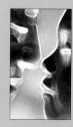

Pattern.jpg   Raffia.jpg   Ruth&Garth.jpg   Hongi.jpg

Basic Start for most New Projects

Just as in a traditional scrapbook all projects start with a blank file. In image editing software programs, this is the same as making a new file.

Remember, when you make your own projects, to enter the page size most suitable to your album or printout. Resolution should be 300 pixels per inch if you want photographic quality prints.

New Page

From the menu choose File > New and enter the dimensions shown below. This creates a new blank file with a white background

Use the Eyedropper tool to sample colors from any image and help co-ordinate your design.

2 From the menu choose Layer > New > Layer to make a new layer above the white background. Name it "Base". Color it with red using the Paintbucket as shown on page 26

The red color used in this example can be set in the Color Picker: R182, G43 and B55.

3 Save the file in Photoshop PSD format. This keeps the layers intact and is the recommended format for saving files while "work is in progress"

Add & Blend a Pattern

Pattern.jpg

The texture for the background paper is created by blending a pattern with the red base layer. A pattern has already been made for you but if you prefer you can take this as a starting point for a new pattern and create your own as described on page 86.

Pattern

Making a pattern this way will not make a perfect repeat. For this project this will not matter as the pattern is subdued and largely covered by other elements.

1 Open the file Pattern.jpg. To see both open files use Window > Images > Tile

2 Drag the pattern onto the red base with the Move tool. Close the Pattern file as it is no longer needed

3 The pattern is too small, so either generate a new one or use Image > Transform > Free Transform, and drag the handles to fill the page. In the example the pattern has also been rotated

Remember to keep the Layers palette open so you can see how your album page is being constructed.

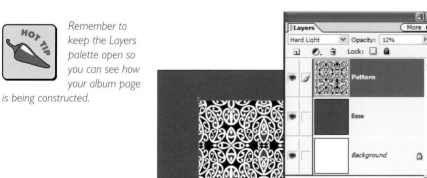

4 Change the blending mode to Hard Light to reveal both the pattern and the underlying layer

5 Lower the Opacity as shown for a more subtle pattern. Save

Add the Main Photo

Ruth&Garth.jpg
© Carolyn Lamb-Miller

All projects are likely to have one or more images within the page. Sometimes one picture is enough, particularly if it is as stunning as this one.

Repeat the Drag Process

1   Open the file Ruth&Garth.jpg. Arrange the open files with the menu command Window > Images > Tile

2   Drag the Ruth&Garth file over to the red patterned background. Close the Ruth&Garth file because it is no longer needed

3   Enlarge the photo slightly with Image > Transform > Free Transform. Your page and the Layers palette will now look something like the example shown below. Your layout is beginning to take shape

Do not alter sizes with Image > Resize > Image Size. This will change everything and not just the photo.

When transforming images hold down the shift key to maintain correct perspective. If you do not, the image will be distorted.

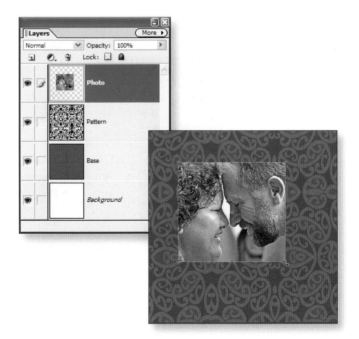

Add a Mat

If you are using software that has guides, such as Photoshop, you will find these a great help for laying out and spacing.

All projects are likely to include several digital elements or embellishments on the page. Here you will make a simple black mat and position it under the photo so that it looks like a frame.

Add a Black Mat

1. Pick the Rectangle tool and drag a rectangle shape a little bigger than the photo – this is why the photograph was positioned and resized first

2. Change the color of the mat to black and position it under the photo. You may have to alter the layer order as shown on page 47

The black mat should extend about ¼ inch (6mm) on three sides and 1 inch (25mm) on the right-hand side of the photo.

3. If the mat or the photo is not the correct size then adjust with Image > Transform > Free Transform. Press the Enter key or the commit button to accept any changes. The image and Layers palette should now look something like this:

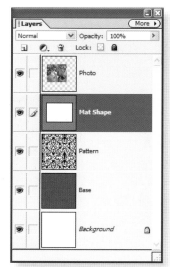

With Shape or Type layers you will often need to Simplify the layer in order to apply some effects. The process turns the "vector graphic" into pixels.

4. Simplify the Mat layer with Layer > Simplify Layer, and add some gentle texture. The example used Noise > Add Noise

Add other Elements

Raffia.jpg

Add the Raffia

1 Open the Raffia.jpg file and drag it onto the album page. You will use this image twice. Position it under the photo, as shown below, and transform it to fit

2 To give a cutout appearance select the unwanted white areas above and below the raffia with the Magic Wand and delete them. (Press Delete or Backspace on the keyboard)

If the black mat is not the correct size it can be transformed again.

3 Duplicate the raffia layer and reposition the copy down the right hand side as shown below. You will have to rotate the copy using Image > Rotate > Layer 90° Left

4 The layout should now look something like this:

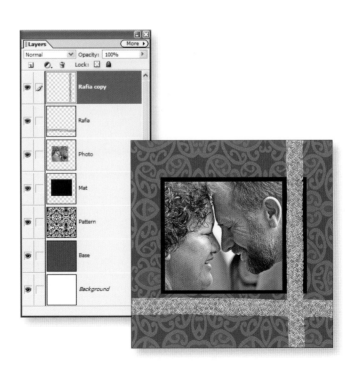

Hongi.jpg

Add the Final Image

1 Repeat the drag process for the Hongi.jpg file illustration. This was once a full color image, but it has been radically adjusted using filters. Reposition it to the bottom right corner of the page

2 Change the blending mode in the Layers palette to Luminosity.... Magic!

3 Select the image and add a red 5-pixel stroke

Add Type

Keep each type element on a separate layer, so that they can be easily moved and changed as your ideas about the page design develop.

Type is very important to scrapbookers and is referred to as journaling. Here you will create strong but simple captions and enhance them with drop shadows to create the illusion of depth.

Type Tool

1 Type the word "Welcome" and position it over the top of the photo. Use a script-type font: the one shown here is called Brush Script and it is found on most computers

2 Type the word "Powhiri" and position it just above the raffia

3 Type the words "Haere mai" and position them just above "Welcome". Change the font colors, position, size and type as you wish. The example uses white and a yellowish color sampled from the raffia. Font sizes are 125 and 175 point

Enhance – Drop Shadows

Finishing Touches

1 To add reality to the layout, add a drop shadow to most of the elements. Make the Raffia layer active and find the Styles and Effects palette. Pick Soft Edge to give the raffia a subtle shadow

2 Repeat for the Raffia copy layer and add a Hard Edge shadow to the three type layers. The stronger shadow gives the illusion that the type is floating above the layout

3 Flatten the image using Layer > Flatten Image, and save it

In Photoshop Elements when you add a drop shadow to the Hongi layer the image returns to its original black and white state. Change the blending mode back to Luminosity to regain the effect. This does not happen if you are using Photoshop.

When Grandpop was a High Flyer

In traditional scrapbooking there are specialist companies that deal entirely with preserving memories. They have very high standards in both the materials they recommend and how memories are presented. One such company is Creative Memories and their website is well worth a look – www.creativememories.com.

One of the greatest dilemmas with family memories is that there is usually such a lot of information. You may not know where to start. Limit yourself to a single idea and your thoughts will be focussed and the images needed rationalized.

Alan Francis is now a farmer in New Zealand. This project tells the story of Alan Francis in another life, as a wireless operator in a Lancaster bomber during the Second World War. The words are provided by Henry, a schoolboy who has just "interviewed" the flyer concerned – his grandpop. With this in mind the typeface chosen and general theme reflects the age and personality of the young writer. The project attempts to develop a sense of excitement and adventure alongside Alan's sad tales. Of very great interest are the logbooks and personal photos that reflect these poignant times.

With many old photos there is a need both to preserve and to restore them. Digital scrapbooking has a very significant advantage in making this easy and importantly the original is not harmed. It is recommended that you scan images at the best quality possible.

Covers

Logbook.jpg

Badge.jpg

Lancaster.jpg

Flag.png

Collect, Sort and Repair

Team

Lancaster

Mates

Alan

Badge

ID Card

Navigate

Logbook

All images © Alan Francis

There are eight images in this project plus a couple of elements for you to create. It is a good idea to work on individual images before starting the main file. In practice the images would be scanned at 16 bit to get the best possible detail and tonal range (check if your scanner can do this). They would then be "corrected" in Photoshop before being converted to 8 bit for "normal" use. The images available for this project, however, are 8 bit and have not been corrected – so there is plenty of work for you to do!

Repair and Renew

Open each file in turn and check what needs to be done to restore or to improve the image. Suggestions are given below.

Team   This photo has been scanned crookedly. Crop and straighten it. Adjust Levels. Try moving the white slider to the left to liven up the tones.

Lancaster   Crop to remove the large white marks on the left and straighten the image. Adjust Levels as shown on page 142. Eliminate dust marks with the Spot Healing Brush.

Mates   Crop to remove excess sky. Remove minor blemishes. Add a 10-pixel white stroke around the edge to provide a border.

Alan   Crop to remove excess background, but leave a border. The image is lacking in contrast. Open the Levels dialog and brighten the image using the white eyedropper as described on page 147. Remove blemishes with the Spot Healing Brush.

Badge   Delete the white edging. To do this open the Layers palette and double-click on the Background layer to create a "real" layer. Select the white space with the Magic Wand and press the Delete key. Save the file in PSD format to preserve transparency. Adjust Levels. Move the white slider to the left to brighten colors.

ID Card   Remove the white background and adjust Levels. Try moving the white slider to the 233 position to lighten the blue.

Navigate   Remove the background and adjust Levels to lighten it.

Logbook   Rotate this and remove the background. This is not so straightforward as the others. Use the Background Eraser and the Polygonal Lasso, taking extra care with the bottom left corner.

Camouflage Background

The file size for this project will be very large. Expect your computer to run slowly.
You may find it advantageous to work on individual elements and assemble them at the end.

The background for this project is a diffuse blue-grey to symbolize both the camouflage colors of the aircraft and the overcast skies of a Europe at war. The blending of the colors needs to be subtle to avoid overpowering the images that will be placed on top. You will employ a little trick to achieve the softness needed.

Double Page Spread – Not Yet!

1 Make a new file only 4 inches high and 6 inches wide

2 Set the foreground color to R215, G222, B231 and the background color to R164, G164, B176 in the Color Picker

By making the Camouflage file small and stretching it, extra softness is achieved and the overlying images are not overpowered.

3 From the menu choose Filter > Render > Clouds. Save the file as Camouflage.tif but keep it open

It is a good idea to rename layers especially when there are many, as in this project.

4 Make a new file suitable for a double page spread

5 Drag the Camouflage file onto the double page spread and stretch (transform) or resize to fit as shown on page 56. Commit the transformation and save the file as Flyer.psd

You may want to close this file temporarily while you make the next element.

6 Drag the images onto the layout. Reposition and resize them as shown on page 174. Lower the opacity of the Logbook layer so that it blends into the background. Save again

Flags – Make them Wave

Flag.png

An important element in this layout is the flag. The original image is static. Give the flag some life and add extra interest to the page.

Wave

The extra space should be transparent.

1   To make the flag look more realistic add texture using Filter > Texturizer. The example uses the settings shown opposite

2   The wave is applied by a Shear filter. This only works horizontally so use Image > Rotate > 90° (left or right is up to you!)

3   To give space for the "wave" increase the Canvas Size by 50%. You only need to increase the Width as shown

4   Apply the filter Distort > Shear. Click on the central straight line to create anchor points and drag to cause the distortion as shown opposite. Click OK to accept the changes. Rotate the flag back to its horizontal position

Set the tools to a low Opacity. Use several light strokes in preference to a single heavy one.

5   It's looking good but a few shadows and highlights are needed to complete the effect, using the Dodge and Burn tools. Pick the Dodge tool and apply smooth brush strokes over the two areas that would naturally catch the light. Be subtle!

6   Change to the Burn tool and repeat the process to add a little more shading near the stars

7   Save the file as Flag2.psd. Drag it onto the main layout, resize and reposition it. Close the Flag2 file

8   Reduce the Opacity of the Flag layer to make it translucent and let the layers beneath partially show through. (On page 174 the Navigate file appears near the top of the flag). Put a gentle Outer Glow around the flag and save

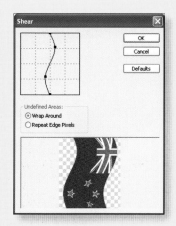

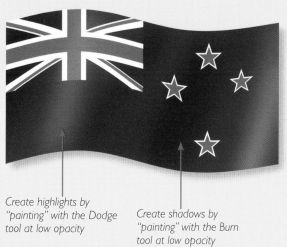

Create highlights by "painting" with the Dodge tool at low opacity

Create shadows by "painting" with the Burn tool at low opacity

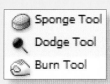

Stitching & additional Elements

In this section you will make a journaling mat and place it beneath the Lancaster photo. This shape will become a mat with a texture reminiscent of the haversacks or packs used by the armed forces.

Canvas Mat

Sample colors for an exact match with the Eyedropper.

1 Open the Lancaster file. You should have already cropped this as suggested on page 168. Drag it onto the main background

2 Make a new layer and call it "Mat". With the Rectangular Marquee tool draw a selection a little bigger than the photo. Fill it with a blue color similar to that of the ID Card

3 Fray the edges of the mat as shown on page 98. This example uses the Texture Comb Brush 1 at a very large 450-point size

4 Add texture to the mat the easy way. Click on the "Lock transparent pixels" button in the Layers palette. Then use Filter > Texture > Texturizer > Burlap

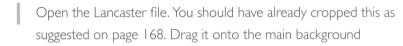

Lock transparent pixels to stop them being changed. A padlock appears in the layer

5 Alter the stack order so that the photo is on top of the mat and adjust the size of the mat to give space for several lines of journaling at the bottom of the photo

Add the effect of stitching with clever use of the Brush Tool.

A Stitch in Time

1 Make a new layer and call it Stitching

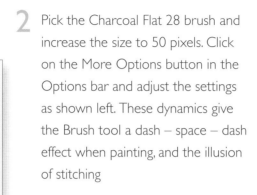

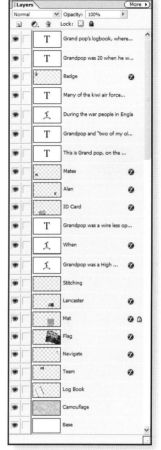

2 Pick the Charcoal Flat 28 brush and increase the size to 50 pixels. Click on the More Options button in the Options bar and adjust the settings as shown left. These dynamics give the Brush tool a dash – space – dash effect when painting, and the illusion of stitching

3 Painting a straight line with a mouse is not easy, but there is a great trick you can use. Click where you want the line to begin. A brush mark appears. Move the mouse to where you want the line to end, hold down the shift key and click again. A completely straight line is drawn with all the dynamics of the brush included. Powerful stuff!

4 This brush is the wrong shape to paint the stitching vertically. Go back into More Options and change the Angle to -90°. Repeat the magic

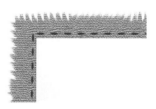

5 Add shadows to all the elements and an Outer Glow to the Badge. Save

Journaling

In Heritage layouts words are very important. They convey a personal message and feeling that the photo alone cannot. It is important to use a typeface that is easily read but also has relevance. Here the font "Marker Felt" is used to reflect the sort of pen used by the schoolboy author of the text.

Grandpop.doc © Henry Francis is available as a Word document or a PDF

All yours, Henry!

1 Open the Grandpop text in a word processor and select point 5. Edit and Copy

In Photoshop draw a text box to contain the text when it is pasted. The bounding box can be resized and the text will reflow within the box. In Photoshop Elements the text arrives as a long unformatted line. It's a chore but you will have to manually apply new formatting.

2 Back in Photoshop Elements pick the Type tool, make an insertion point on the main file and choose Edit > Paste

3 Reformat and position the text. Pick a suitable typeface and color. Repeat for all the other sections of text

4 Add a main caption. For a bit of schoolboy fun use Warp Text, as shown on page 103, to make the caption look like an aeroplane. Save the file and close it. Thank you, Henry!

Celebration – Birthday Girl

In this chapter you get a chance to see how your skills compare with those of the experts. Clara Wallace of Matter of Scrap has prepared a special layout for the finale. However, don't be disappointed if your layout doesn't look exactly like Clara's. You may not have access to the same fonts and your software may give slightly different results. Then there is the little matter of experience! This exercise was prepared using Photoshop.

Covers

Chapter Twelve

Merrygoround.jpg

MerrygoroundEND.tif

Hand-Textured Papers

The Paisley shape for Clara's file was created from a dingbat font and is available from www.houseoflime.com. Download the file Paisley or Paisley 2 if you want your own work to look similar to Clara's original. This exercise uses a freely-available custom shape.

The background to this layout has two papers. The base paper is covered with a swirling stencil-like pattern. Overlapping this at the bottom of the page is a distressed "dot" pattern paper. Both are made in a similar way.

Base Paper

1 Make a new file 12 inches square, the size of a traditional album

2 Add a new layer and call it "Base". Fill this with a salmon color. This example uses R148, G190, B152. Add gentle texture with the Noise filter and Filter > Artistic > Palette Knife (Settings 5,2,7)

3 The pattern is hand-applied with a brush created from a shape. Draw a shape in red using Custom Shape Floral Ornament 1, shown left. Rasterize this layer

4 Select the shape with the Magic Wand and apply a 3-pixel black stroke. Delete the selected area. If you turn off the visibility of all other layers, the shape should now look like this:

5 With the Rectangular Marquee tool drag a box over the shape and use Edit > Define Brush Preset. Give the new brush a name such as "Flower Outline". This now appears in the Brushes palette. If this is the case delete the Shape 1 layer – it has done its job

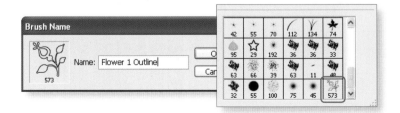

6 Pick the new brush and set the dynamics. Pay particular attention to the Spacing, Size Jitter and Hue Jitter

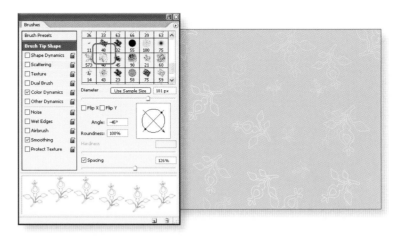

7 Make a new layer. Call it "Floral" and paint the page. For added interest change the brush dynamics and repeat the process. Change the blending mode in the Layers palette to Screen

Green Paper

1 Make a new layer and call it Green paper. Make a selection of the bottom third of this layer and color it green

2 Add gentle texture. In this example Noise was followed by Filter > Sketch > Water paper with settings of 31, 57 and 85

Erase the edge of the green paper to help the two papers blend.

3 Pick the Eraser and the Stencil Sponge – Twirl brush. Either paint freehand over the green background or alter the brush dynamics to give 125% spacing. The effect is to partially erase the green layer to show the salmon color beneath. It should give the impression of animal hoof prints

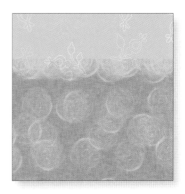

Glassy Elements

An important part of Clara's layout are glassy, chrome and wood elements. These should be made as separate files before being dragged onto the main image. This section concentrates on the glassy elements.

Reflective Moment

The foreground and background colors are set in the Color Picker. Used here are R244, G0, B103 and R247, G39, B185.

1 Make a new file. For the larger button use a page size of 3 x 1 inches. Set the foreground and background colors as shown

2 Pick the Rounded Rectangle tool. Set the Radius to 25 px (pixels), and drag out the rectangle shape

3 In the Layer Styles dialog set the options as shown below

Use the Gradient Editor to set the Gradient Overlay colors to those you have already chosen as the foreground and background colors.

Click here to see the Gradient Editor

This color is R249, G198, B118

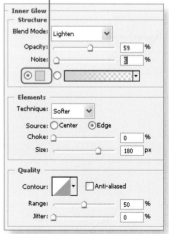

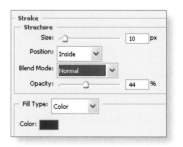

For added softening of the highlight add a Gaussian Blur. Here this was applied at a Radius of 2.6.

4   This gives a shape looking like the one above

5   To create the highlight draw another rounded rectangle but with a Radius set to 15 pixels. Rasterize this layer

6   Pick the Blur tool and set the size to 65 pixels. Smudge the highlight layer at the left and right edges as shown. Reduce the Opacity of this layer to around 30%. Your button should be taking shape

7   Type the word "Fabulous" and make sure the type layer is below the highlight layer (Shape 2)

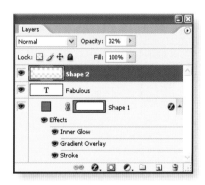

8   Discard the Background layer and merge the rest. Save the file in PSD or PNG format to preserve the transparency

9   Drag the merged file onto the main layout and resize it

Photo Correction & Enhancement

Merrygoround.jpg
© Clara Wallace

Virtually all photos can be enhanced with editing software. The main photo for this project is no different. Additionally this receives subtle creative changes.

Open up the Shadows

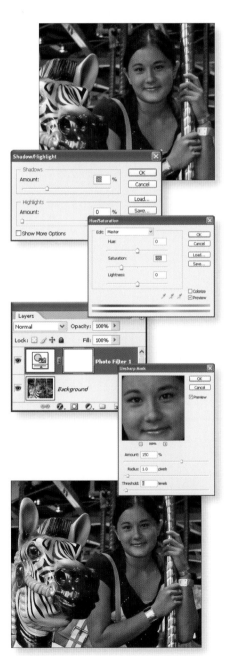

1 Open the file Merrygoround.jpg and notice that the shadows to the right are a little dark. Use Image > Adjustments > Shadow/Highlight. By default most images appear too light. Adjust as shown

In Photoshop Elements navigate to Enhance > Adjust Lighting > Shadows/Highlights.

2 To enhance the image Clara reduced the overall saturation with the Hue/Saturation command

Avoid deep shadows at the taking stage by using flash as explained on page 141.

3 To add more warmth an 81A Photo Filter was applied using an Adjustment layer as shown on page 147

4 Finally sharpen the image using Filter > Sharpen > Unsharp Mask. Save it

5 Flatten the layers and then drag the photo onto the main layout

Animal Text

For the large captions you need to use a bold font. The one used here is Cooper Black. The word "Animals" is not in a straight line and one letter is overlapping the photo.

Experiment with different fonts. The one below is Bauhaus. It doesn't need much imagination to be able to see all sorts of animals in the letters.

Zoo Time

1 Type the word "ANIMALS" in white. Rasterize the type layer to convert the letters to pixels

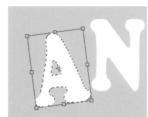

2 Select the letter "A" with the Magic Wand and then use Edit > Free Transform. Move the letter and perhaps rotate it a little. Repeat this step for the other letters

Hold down the shift key to select multiple letters, or uncheck the Contiguous button in the Options bar.

3 Enhance each letter – add a 10-pixel black stroke

4 Select all the remaining white areas. Pick the Brush tool and paint stripes at random across the letters. Clara set the brush shape to alter in size throughout the stroke, a bit like an animal's tail. You can do this by altering the brush dynamics as shown on page 95

If you do not want to make your own, the brush is called clara-zebrastripes. abr. It can be downloaded free from www.ineasysteps.com.

Finishing Touches

Your page should be looking fantastic. A few extras are needed before the page is complete and these are detailed below. It's now time to compare your work with that of the expert! Hopefully you are pleased with your progress. Good luck with your future projects.

The border decoration is created by making a brush from a twirl custom shape. Alter the brush dynamics to create as much overlap or spacing as needed. The edges were darkened with the Burn tool

Photograph has a slight bevel/emboss applied to give a realistic look

Freehand shadow under the border using a 58-pixel drop shadow brush. Gaussian blur applied and opacity adjusted

Text added around the photo using a font such as Courier or American Typewriter. Lots of "grungy" typewriter fonts are available on the internet

Drop shadow on the "Fabulous" element is pink instead of black – because the element is translucent

Increase the drop shadows for the glassy 2s, since the elements are realistically higher and not flat. Chrome elements are discussed on page 118

The word "Party" simulates rub-on type and also overlaps the photo. It is slightly offset to emphasize the depth difference between the photo and the paper. Make a selection with the Polygon Lasso and put on a new layer. Put this new layer above the photo in the stack

The Adobe web site has many great resources. In particular the Studio Exchange has lots of freebies from other users. If you are having difficulty making chrome, wood or glass elements then this is the place to go. The July element is typical of the resources available. Customize these with your own text and additional layer styles

References & Additional Resources

This book alone is unlikely to answer all your scrapbooking, digital photography, design and software questions. Don't panic! There is much additional help and support easily available.

It may sound boring, but start with the Help files that came with the software. These are a superb resource and will solve a lot of your problems. Many have additional tutorials to further the development of your skills.

If you surf the internet, visit some of the many websites dedicated to both digital and traditional scrapbooking. They are a great source of inspiration and often have freebies to give away; many are also geared up to sell digital elements that may be beyond your present skills to create. Don't forget that many sites also have user forums that allow you to chat with fellow enthusiasts and exchange scrapbooking ideas.

Covers

Chapter Thirteen

Help

There are times when things will happen and no explanation will be found on these pages. In this case try Help > Photoshop Elements Help. Not only is there a comprehensive listing of all commands and tools; there's also a full glossary and more tutorials to help your understanding. Go ahead and explore – you will be surprised how useful this can be. You are also encouraged to see what is available by clicking on the Online Support option and looking at Photoshop Elements Online.

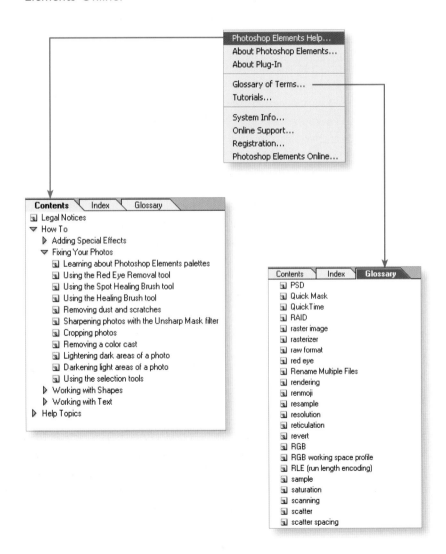

Downloading Images

Downloading from the Internet

Follow a similar procedure when downloading digital elements from scrapbooking websites.

All the files and images for the exercises and projects in this book can be downloaded from www.ineasysteps.com. The images are stored as compressed zip files, which need to be extracted. The procedure for Windows is described below. The steps may change with different operating systems.

Before starting it is strongly suggested that you make a folder on the computer to accept the downloaded files. By default this will be the My Documents folder but you can put them anywhere you like. You may wish to use the Organizer within Photoshop Elements.

Go to the website, find this book and click on the download button. The exact file location is www.ineasysteps.com/books/?1840783036. In Windows a dialog box appears asking if you want to open or save the files. Choose Save. Browse to the location of your choice. When the download is complete go to the folder, right-click and pick Extract All. The extraction wizard starts. Next choose a location for the extracted images – this could be the same folder or a new one.

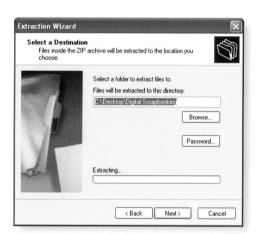

Downloading from Memory Cards & Cameras

There are several ways to get images from A to B, from your camera to the computer. The simplest way is to insert the film card into a card reader, open the image folder and drag the files to the new location. Unfortunately this procedure seems to fill beginners with trepidation and so software manufacturers have come up with automated solutions.

If you use Windows a dialog box appears whenever you connect a camera or card reader. If you have Photoshop Elements installed the Adobe Photo Downloader may also appear at the same time. If you don't want either of these you can turn them off in Preferences.

Edit >
Preferences >
Camera or Card
Reader.

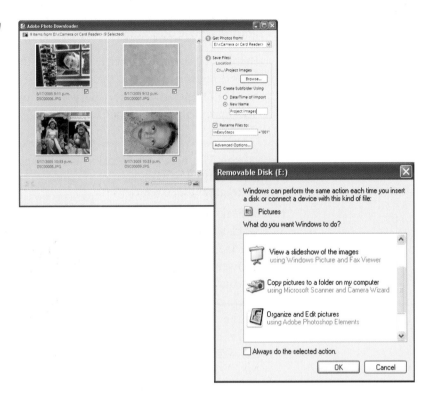

Both downloaders work in essentially the same way. There are a variety of options to set: the model of your camera, the location of the card and the destination for the images. If your camera does not appear as a choice on the menu, make sure that the camera is connected and turned on. It is always a good idea to create a new folder for each new set of photos and give them a name.

If you don't want all the photos on your camera or card reader, deselect the photos you don't want. After the photos have been transferred, you'll be asked if you'd like to delete them from the camera or card reader. Photos that you didn't transfer will not be deleted.

Scrapbooking Websites

There are so many internet sites dealing with scrapbooking that it is impossible to list them all. Below is a cross-section of sites that have proved useful when compiling this book. Some sites deal only with traditional scrapbooking but are still a useful source of ideas and inspiration for all scrapbookers. Others have a speciality – e.g. fonts, poetry etc. Take a look, follow links to other sites and be amazed at what your fellow scrapbookers get up to.

Try doing a search on Google for "Free Fonts".

Useful Sites

www.matterofscrap.com
www.promos4digiscrappers.com
www.digitalfreebies.com
www.houseoflime.com
www.scrapjazz.com
www.scrapbook-bytes.com
www.playonelements.com
www.scrapbookin-annie.co.nz
www.loriweb.pair.com
www.digitalscrapbookplace.com
www.scrapbook-elements.com
www.epson.com (search for Print Lab series)
www.scrapfriends.us
www.escrappers.com
www.scrapbookingdownunder.com
www.mangelsdesigns.com
www.cottagearts.net

Sites for Fonts

www.desktoppub.about.com/od/freefonts
www.letteringdelights.com
www.typenow.net

File Formats

One of the most confusing options you have when saving files is the choice of format. Most imaging software offers numerous options, but there are only three or four that you really need to get your head around when you are new to digital scrapbooking.

TIF or TIFF
The name stands for Tagged Image File Format, but don't let that put you off. This is a standard and universal file format that can easily be read by different software and different computers. TIF is a good choice to maintain the integrity and quality of your images. It is recommended that you archive all your scrapbook albums, pages and projects in TIF format. You should also use this format when saving scanned images.

JPEG
This is the normal format used by consumer digital cameras and is also recommended when attaching image files to emails. Use JPEG format when you want to reduce file sizes but be aware that the format compresses files and in doing so removes some data (lossy compression) that can never be recovered. As such it is not recommended that you use this format when archiving projects and albums – use TIF instead. JPEG is short for Joint Photographic Experts Group.

PSD
This is the native format of Photoshop and Photoshop Elements and stands for Photoshop Document. Save files in this format when you are "experimenting" or have "work in progress". This is especially important if you have layered files, as the format keeps all elements intact. When you have completely finished editing, squash or flatten all layers together and save the document as a TIF file. The layered PSD file can then be discarded.

PNG
Portable Network Graphics (PNG) format is used for lossless compression and for display of images on the web when transparency and smooth edges are needed. For scrapbookers PNG behaves in a very similar way to layered PSD files. Because PNG files are smaller in size than PSD ones, it is commonly used by resellers of digital files on the internet.

Index

S

T

U

V

W

Z